MW00889509

PTSD SAVED
MY LIFE

Herman L Williams with Wyvonne Page

Copyright © 2017, by Page Turners, LLC.
Published by Page Turners, LLC
Fort Mill, South Carolina
Email: Hermanator1.hw@gmail.com
All rights reserved. No part of this book may be reproduced or transmitted in any form or by any means, electronic or mechanical, including photocopying, recording, or by any information storage and retrieval system, without permission from the publisher.
Disclaimer by Herman Williams: This book is my autobiography. While most names and places are accurate to the best of my recollection, some names have been changed to respect and protect their true identity. I apologize if any information herein is taken offensively or in a derogatory way.

ISBN: 1548332410
ISBN: 9781548332419
Cover Design, Fireball Press, Columbus, OH.
Books Printed by Create Space, United States of America

ACKNOWLEDGMENTS

DURING MY LIFE'S journey, my Divine Creator has placed numerous people in my path who have touched me in a multitude of ways. Certainly more than I can mention. The following, however, I must acknowledge:

To my beloved grandparents, McKinley and Estella Williams who I called "Mama" and "Daddy," and my biological parents, Cora Mae Williams and James Small.

To my beloved children, Francine, Twanda, Renese, Maurice, Kelvin and Jerry; **grandchildren**, Marcus, James, Cameronne, Taylor, Nyla, Mary, Alexis, Janasia, Learah, Deron, Deandre, Kevin, Jr. Deandre, and **Great Grandchildren**, Masen, Emmett, Jayda, Tameyah, and Laniyah.

To my beloved wife, Viola, who has been my 'rock.' We have survived more than 40 years, baby. Thank you for your love and putting up with me. ☺

To Liberty High School, all my former teachers and a special thanks to my English and typing teacher Mrs. Glover and Coach Ed Starling.

To the United States Marine Corps, for teaching me to never give up, there is no such thing as can't be done - Anything is possible.

To my attorney, George Penfield, the man I'd gladly take a bullet for - in my finger. ☺

Veterans Administration Medical Center - Brecksville, Ohio, Therapist Anita Martin Kellon, MSN. RNC., and Dr. David Liebling, M.D.

To Wyvonne Page, my book writer. Taking on my book project is a true testament of your generous spirit which transcends the boundaries of humanity. I truly appreciate your dedication and your extraordinary patience during this endeavor.

To my copy editors, George Penfield, Bob and Barbara Smith, and Malcolm Smith. Thank you for your invaluable input.

There are far too many others to list by name, but each of you know the purpose you have served in my life and likewise, the purpose I have served in yours. Please know that I am eternally thankful for your love and support.

To: _Bob_

From: _Herman Williams_

Thank you for your support of my autobiography. Considering that my Creator has brought me this far, through countless adversities, I believe I am fulfilling a major purpose by sharing candid events of my life, before and after being diagnosed with PTSD. I hope you will be inspired.

The
Hermanator!

PREFACE

Post-war veterans return to their homes with a suitcase filled with belongings. Many, however, will carry home invisible baggage. Ignorance is not-bliss when the consequences can be fatal. According to statistics from the U.S. Department of Veterans Affairs, approximately 20 veterans commit suicide each day. More than 7,000 veterans committed suicide during 2014. If these figures seems alarming, then you owe it to yourself and your loved ones to discover any invisible baggage that you may have brought home from the war.

For more than 25 years, Herman "Jerry" Williams has made frequent visits to the Veterans Administration Medical Center, both in-patient and out-patient, in his quest to cope and recover from his Post Traumatic Stress Disorder (PTSD). His success, although short of 100%, has evolved from patient to peer support facilitator at the Louis Stokes Cleveland VA Medical Center, Cleveland, Ohio. Herman is "one who knows," and uses his own experiences to help new veterans seeking treatment for PTSD.

Filed away in Herman's portfolio are numerous certificates of recognition for his service as a VA peer support facilitator which he keeps in his man-cave.

Herman can be found in attendance at various recognition ceremonies for veterans throughout northern Ohio. Attending events such as the annual reenactment of D-Day in Conneaut, has opened doors to meet new and wonderful people with similar interests.

The Wall Street Journal published an article about Herman in the November 20, 2014 issue. On October 24, 2015, he received recognition from Congress of the United States for his service in the United States Marine Corps.

Herman accepts an occasional offer to speak to various groups, schools and events sharing his journey with PTSD and urging veterans who show signs of PTSD to seek help.

Over the years, Herman has been approached to share his story. It has taken many years of treatment in order to reach a comfort level that would allow him to relive the memories and put pen to paper. Finally, with courage, truth and an unwavering desire to help his fellow veterans, this long awaited autobiography is published. Sit back and follow along as Herman "Jerry" Williams shares his journey of discovering his invisible baggage and how the discovery itself saved his life.

Herman hopes, *PTSD Saved My Life*, will inspire post-war veterans to take that leap, not off the bridge, but to a Veterans Administration treatment center for diagnosis and treatment. If not for yourself, then do it for your family and loved ones. Do it in honor of the veterans who committed suicide, thus lost the PTSD battle before taking advantage of the opportunity to rid themselves of the demons of PTSD. Do it for those who turned to crime during their anguish and are now spending time incarcerated. Do it for those veterans who were killed in Vietnam whose names are now engraved on the Vietnam Memorial Wall, located in Washington, D. C. Just do it!

According to the Department of Mental Health and Human Services, PTSD was officially recognized as a disorder in 1980, more than ten years after Herman completed his tour of duty in Vietnam. Although he spent many years suffering, PTSD was recognized in time to save his life, and for that he is eternally grateful.

CHAPTER 1

——— ▲ ▲ ▲ ———

THE CONCEPTION OF my long venturesome journey from the coalfields of West Virginia, to the battlefields of Vietnam, took hold on the day the U.S. Air Force recruiter came to Liberty High. I sat in the hard wooden chair and listened intently as he described all the benefits and opportunities. I gazed with adoration at the recruiter's starched uniform and mirror-shiny boots. For a young skinny black boy growing up between two hills in Williamson, West Virginia, my options for a rewarding career within the city limits had been few. But now, the sensations in my mind were dancing with anticipation.

In my bed that night, I tossed and turned. Distracted by excitement and anticipation, I just couldn't sleep. Instead, I allowed my mind free reign to skim over the highlights of my final and most exciting year of high school.

The year was 1966, and the Liberty High Yellowjackets were working their way to the state class 'A' basketball championship game. It was a very exciting time for Coach Ed Starling and the entire Liberty High basketball team. Little did we know that a strategic plan was being implemented to close our all black school. And I do mean all black, students and staff alike. I would later come to understand that closing the school was enacted by the Civil Rights movement of the '60s. I am convinced that the powers-that-be who controlled the Board of Education, and issued the order to close my school, never expected the Yellowjackets basketball team to rise up to stardom during that final year. It was a totally unexpected phenomenon.

Two days before Liberty met the Lions from the predominantly white high school over at Piedmont, Coach Starling called a "come to Jesus" pow wow. To each and every player, he called out a compliment coupled with some strong demands. "Williams! you're important to this team, and you'd better be ready if and when your number gets called!"

"Yes, sir!" I replied with unwavering confidence.

At 5 foot 9, I was next to the shortest player on a team whose tallest member soared to 6 foot 3. However, there were no shortcomings in my heart. No one was more ready than me, especially after all that bench warming during the season. If only I'd been more than a sub waiting eagerly for that glorious opportunity when Coach Starling would call me onto the court.

"Well alright," said coach. "Let's Get It Done!"

Coach Starling obsessed over the championship like all of history depended on it. You could see the fire in his large brown eyes as he pleaded with the players. "For the next two days, please stay out of trouble, so we can beat those Lions! Alright?"

The team marched from the locker room chanting, "Beat those Lions, beat those Lions, beat those Lions!"

On the night of the game, the Yellowjackets lost to the Lions, 58-55. In spite of the loss, the entire school and community were still filled with pride. I wish I could have taken more of the credit, but the only jump shots I made were from the bench where I remained throughout the entire game.

PICTURED ABOVE is the 1966 Liberty High School Yellowjackets who were the Class A state runner-up that season. Front row, l to r, head coach Ed Starling, Paul Joyce, James Clayburn, Ronald "Doc" Blackwell, Jerry Williams, and Chester Woods. Back row, l to r, principal Harry Joyce, manager Vernon Murrell, James "J.T." Hairston, James Hambrick, William Dawson, Jesse Carter, Norman Phillips, Donnie Wilkerson, Danny Belcher (partially hidden) and manager Jerome Thorn. (Photo courtesy of Norman Phillips)

Yellowjackets Basketball Team pictured above.
Herman "Jerry" Williams, jersey # 33.

▲ ▲ ▲

Coach Starling was skilled in several sports. In addition to basketball, he coached football, baseball and track. I lettered in all four, but my all-time favorite was football. As the team's right corner linebacker, there was no bench warming for me.

The Yellowjacket football players were gearing up to play the number one team in the state, Crum High School. Crum had always given Liberty a hard time and Coach Starling had warned us before the game. "Those boys are bad with a capital "B," and I don't want you to underestimate them. You hear me, Williams?"

"Yes, sir," I eagerly responded.

On the night of the game, I gave chase to Crum's number one halfback, Singleton. At the 25 yard line, I started the chase purposely giving Singleton enough space because I wanted my friends to see how fast I could run. I was also striving to make a sensational play, in that order. As Singleton sped to the 40 yard line, I made a leap for his back. To my dismay, I fell short and landed right into a mud hole. What a sight! Hilarious for some, humiliating for me. Coach Starling was nothing short of furious. "Williams, you knew that ground was soggy, and didn't I tell you not to underestimate that boy?" Coach growled in my face. All I could do was hang my head in disappointment. That day, I learned two valuable lifelong lessons. Never underestimate the opposing team, and keep my ego in check!

Crum won the game by only a few points, but I'm sure they will long remember the Yellowjackets who gave them one hell of a game.

In later years, Coach Starling went on to become the Assistant Athletic Director at Marshall University in Huntington, West Virginia.

▲ ▲ ▲

Another memorable event that occurred during my senior year was attending the homecoming game between Ohio's Wilberforce University and West Virginia State. When Coach Starling announced that he had made arrangements to take the whole team, we went crazy with excitement. The bus ride to West Virginia State was over an hour long each way, and the high energy and chatter was non-stop.

Aside from the sheer excitement of the game, just being on the grounds of a college campus pumped my veins and imagination for a future outside Williamson, West Virginia. After all, facing the grim facts, there weren't many careers that a black man could dream of back in the '60s. Perhaps, had I inherited my grandfather McKinley's 6 foot 7 inch frame, playing ball may have been a strong possibility. But, that was not the case for me.

CHAPTER 2

——— ▲▲▲ ———

My grandparents, McKinley and Estella Williams, whom I called Daddy and Mama, had always hoped the right door would open for me, outside of Williamson, West Virginia. Neither wanted me to follow in Daddy's footsteps, and most certainly, I had no aspirations of suffering through the occupational hazards of the coal mining industry - not after seeing how the mines had sucked the life out of Daddy.

Daddy had spent many years as a coal miner in the small town of Cinderella, West Virginia, located ten miles from Williamson. Cinderella was a shipping point on the Norfolk and Western Railway for coal in the Cinderella mines, as referenced by (Wikipedia). Like thousands who made their careers working the mines, it was a treacherous life for Daddy. I can still recall the piercing sound of the whistle blowing that indicated an emergency had occurred in the mine. Families would literally stop whatever they were doing and start running to the tipple of the mine to see what had happened, who was hurt and how they could help. Whenever the whistle blew, it was an "all-hands" call for the entire community, including the women who were needed to prepare as much food as they could to feed the responders busy with the rescue mission. Even the children took part in the rescue, running errands back and forth for the adults.

Thank God the whistle never blew on account of Daddy. His demise, like thousands of others, had slowly developed over a span of many years due to inhaling coal dust from the confines of the coal mines. Eventually, black lung and poor circulation lead to the amputation of Daddy's right leg. As if that wasn't heartrending enough, his left leg was amputated a few years later.

▲ ▲ ▲

After Daddy could no longer work in the Cinderella Mines, the entire Williams family relocated. Several of my uncles, McKinley Jr., Carl, Alonzo, and Pete enlisted in various branches of the military. Other family members scattered to Washington, D.C.; Bridgeport, Connecticut; Staten Island, New York; and Cleveland, Ohio. My biological mother, Cora Mae Williams, decided to move to Warren, Ohio, leaving my younger sister, Alice, and me to be raised by our grand-parents. Mama and Daddy were two extra special people. They already had a large family with fifteen children of their own, yet they still had enough room in their hearts for Alice and me. Truly, I am grateful for the sacrifices they ob-viously had to make in order to care for so many children.

I was just seven years old when Mama and Daddy moved us to Williamson, West Virginia, also known as the "Heart of the Billion Dollar Coalfield." This name was given due to the prosperous coal mining industry that began after the Norfolk and Western Railway brought its main line through the city of Williamson. The city later became a center for all the coal operations in southern West Virginia, as referenced at http://www.cityofwilliamson.org/history of-city-hall.html. Williamson is also home of the historic Hatfield and McCoy House, a country inn located in the heart of Hatfield McCoy feud country.

Williamson was nobody's country town. It was the "big" city where commerce and entertainment came together. Folks from the surrounding towns would come to Williamson on the weekends, especially the miners. Williamson is where they spent their money on shopping, dining, theaters, gambling, party girls and more. Everything that a big city had to offer could be found in Williamson.

Although Williamson has a "rich" history, I didn't personally know anybody who got rich from working in the mines. I did, however, have the opportunity to know several prominent black business owners. Down on Third Avenue is where you could find Bob's Tavern and Fred's Place; prominent black doctors, Thompson, Warren and Whitticoe; and the dentist, Dr. Clark.

I still recall the day Mama sent me running to fetch Dr. Warren to deliver my baby sister, Margaret. It seemed like I ran a mile before I reached the doctor's front door, out of breath. "Dr. Warren, come quick!" I panted. "Mama said, the baby is coming." In reality, the distance was about ten city blocks. Aside from the doctor bringing my new baby sister into this world, I still marvel at the image of him running the entire ten blocks right next to me with his black doctor's bag swinging in his hand.

A major hang-out for all the kids in Williamson was Dr. Whitticoe's drug store which had a soda fountain and various flavors of ice cream. The history of Dr. Whitticoe goes back to the days when he would ride his buckskin, Fancy, to see his patients in their homes. That was before my time, but I do remember that Fancy was kept in a barn next to the Liberty Elementary School. On occasion, Fancy would take a notion to jump the fence and go "willy-nilly" down Vinson Street. I used to fantasize about catching that old horse and riding him around town before taking him back to his barn.

▲ ▲ ▲

Third Avenue was truly the hub of activity for the blacks in Williamson. If anyone doubted its prominence, it became evident after John F. Kennedy graced the sidewalks with his presence while campaigning for President of the United States in 1960. JFK's photo was captured in front of Flora's Place where I used to gaze longingly through the glass countertop at her plates of food on display. Chittlins, collards and corn bread, mac n cheese – boy oh boy, I couldn't wait until I was grown up and had my own money so I too could sample some of Ms. Flora's soul food. I yearned to sit alongside the grown folks who sat at the tables smacking their lips and lickin' their fingers, and exclaiming how good was Ms. Flora's food.

I was also proud to have known some of the old-timers who shook hands with JFK, like Archie Bland, the gentleman seated on the chair in the picture below.

I was also acquainted with Mr. Fred Strauter from Fred's nightclub, and his daughter, Bonnie. After shaking hands with JFK, Mr. Fred asked him if he could wait for his daughter to come out and say, "Hello." Mr. Fred was so excited and honored that JFK obliged his request and waited for Bonnie.

JFK was indeed the buzz for days. I was only thirteen at the time, not yet old enough to vote, but I was proud just the same when he was actually elected President of the United States.

▲ ▲ ▲

After I had made a few friends with some of the local boys my age, I would humor them with stories of my life back in Cinderella. One day when the temperatures were scorching and my friends and I longed to cool off in the water, I started bragging about the Cinderella Dam where I used to swim, and the water moccasin that had chased my ass out of the water. When I look back, I can only say that I must have had one heck of a persuasive persona, for I was able to convince those boys to play hooky from school and walk the full ten miles so I could show them the dam. I was also hoping we'd get a glimpse of the snakes. Sho'nuff we had a blast that day, swimming in the dam, looking over each other's shoulders and teasing that the menacing moccasins were lurking under water. Unfortunately, we lost track of time, and back at the home fronts our parents had started to worry. Whether the good time we had that day was worth the whipping we got that night cannot be measured, but for sure, that was our last journey together to the Cinderella Dam.

CHAPTER 3

——— ▲▲▲ ———

MY HIGH SCHOOL English teacher, Mrs. Glover used to emphasize that anything can be easy if you like it well enough and work hard at it. Attending school in Williamson was like that for me. In fact, I loved school. My teachers, especially Mrs. Glover and Coach Starling, took a genuine interest in me. To this day, I still hold them in my heart with fond memories. I loved to read and above all other subjects, my favorite was science. I can still name the nine planets and the four gases in the atmosphere.

Most times, I was a happy-go-lucky kid and considered the class clown, but, like most people, I had my shortcomings. I could have everybody laughing during homeroom and draw a crowd for a fist fight during lunch. Most fights were instigated by my friends who provoked me simply because they could. They knew I had a hot temper that didn't take much to boil over. I was especially an *easy* prey when playing the dozens, a game where two or more spewed out insults about each other, particularly negative comments about our parents. Perhaps it was because Mama and Daddy were my grandparents, and I felt they should be regarded with the highest of respect.

In spite of my shortcomings, I was voted class president during my senior year. Aside from that major accomplishment, some of the happiest and most memorable years of my school days were experienced during my senior year.

▲ ▲ ▲

Like all the teachers at Liberty, Mrs. Lomax was multi-talented. Not only was she our homeroom teacher, she taught biology, science and music. Liberty had an annual tradition whereby the senior homeroom class would perform a play. During the class year of 1966, Mrs. Lomax decided to direct the musical, *The Toy Maker.* She also played the piano for the play.

All the male students vied for the leading role of the toy maker, but the lucky guy selected was my friend, Terry Warren. Deep down I really wanted that part, but my reputation as the class clown had made the decision real easy for Mrs. Lomax, when she cast me as the clown which had a singing part. I had a good memory and quickly learned the lyrics to "A Merry Clown Am I." In addition to learning my own lines and song for the play, I learned Terry's and my friend Ronald's, as well. The play was held in the school's auditorium and the community came out in droves. Our performance was so well done we were asked to perform it again.

Pictured above is the cast for the "Toy Maker." I'm number six, starting from the left. Since the senior class was "short staffed," so to speak, a couple of girls from the junior class participated in the play.

Most days my dress attire was jeans and short sleeve shirts. However, being the class president and knowing our photo would be published in the '66 yearbook, I'd made the suggestion that we all dress up. I wanted to prove that the class clown knew how to dress up when the occasion called for it. Actually, I was trying to dress like my uncles who brought the trends back from Cleveland, Ohio. Only thing missing was my hair-do. I liked the processed style, but couldn't erase a horrible image from my mind. I'd been hanging out with a group of teenagers in the back yard of a "wanna be" barber who was applying a white smelly cream onto the head of a trusting soul. Within minutes after the cream was applied, the dude suddenly sprang up out of the chair running and screaming, arms flailing because the lye was scorching his scalp. The commotion even startled a dog sleeping nearby which took off in fright. After this jolt to my senses, I never did muster up the courage to pursue the processed hair style.

▲ ▲ ▲

During my last year of high school, my academic focus took a slight dive. Girls and sports were the culprit. Six months into the school year, I had the pleasure of meeting Sandra Franklin. I believed it was fate that Sandra and I met. She didn't attend Liberty High like the other girls I knew, but she and her sister Janet attended as many of Liberty's basketball games as they could hike a ride to. That wasn't easy being that they lived in Matewan, more than twenty miles from Williamson.

Our first meeting was following one of Liberty's games. Terry Warren and I had been hanging out when we ran into Martin West and a beautiful girl I'd not seen around town before. Clearly, Martin and I were not the best of friends, and the plan that was conjuring up in my mind would certainly sever any thoughts of such in the future.

"Hey guys," Martin said. "Meet my girl, Sandra." Martin was all smiles as he introduced us. "We're heading to the movie theater," he went on. Sandra's smile was absolutely radiant as she extended her hand to Terry's and then into mine. Suddenly, the decision was made, if only in my mind, to accompany her and Martin to the theater. Elvis was hot back in those days, and his movie, *Paradise, Hawaiian Style,* was showing on the big screen. Stalking from two rows behind, I sat and waited for Martin to leave. Quickly, I slid into the seat he had just vacated. Sandra protested with a smile, "Boy, Martin will be right back."

"Don't matter. All I need to know is how to contact you later."

Before Martin could return with arms filled with popcorn and sodas, I had convinced Sandra to give up her phone number. I probably should have watched the movie to see what other smooth moves I might learn from Elvis, but at that moment, I had just scored big and was walking out singing, *"when you're out on a date, Jerry stalks till you walk away…"*

With no cars of our own to drive, the twenty or so miles between Sandra's house and mine made it difficult to see each other as much as we wanted. Our phone calls, however, were long, frequent, and hot. By the time the opportunity came about that we could see each other, which was few and far between, we were two very excited teenagers. On a couple of occasions when we had a few minutes to spare before her mother came home, let's just say things got pretty steamy, pretty fast. Sandra and I had a future, I just knew. They called that "Puppy Love."

Aside from my budding romance with Sandra, my mind and body was preoccupied with the championship basketball game coming up. All I could think about was whether I'd get a chance to play. I was even praying to God that somehow, someway, something would happen to one of the other players. Nothing critical, but just minor enough that Coach Starling would allow me the chance to fill in for once. After all, it was my last year to play high school ball.

In Daddy's condition, he wasn't able to show his support by attending the games, but he loved to listen to the recaps when I got home. Many times, I headed home immediately following after school sports practice, and while helping Mama with his care, I'd fill him up with all the play-by-play details.

Daddy was a tall proud man and didn't want any help from anybody. Sometimes though, he'd grow weary and allow me to help him get in and out of his wheelchair. He'd also allow me to shave him with one of those fancy double edge razors that Uncle Ferbee had sent from Cleveland. During those times, I'd pretend I was a barber, and he was my favorite client. Even though I'd lather him up with plenty of shaving cream, there was still the occasional slip of my hand that ultimately drew specs of blood from Daddy's course skin. The first time my hand slipped under Daddy's chin, I immediately slapped some Old Spice aftershave on him. That mistake I only made once. To see Daddy, with no legs, almost jump out of his chair is an image I will never forget. It took a few minutes for his skin to cool down from the alcohol burn, during

which time I repeated over and over, "I'm sorry, Daddy,
I'm sorry." Fortunately Daddy regained his trust in me,
and from that point on, whenever I *accidently* nicked him,
I'd shake some baby powder in the palm of my hand and
tenderly pat it on his skin.

Daddy also loved to smoke his cigars and puff on his
pipe. Sometimes he'd allow me to fill his pipe with his favorite Prince Albert tobacco and light it for him. I enjoyed
this privilege tremendously, and was quite distraught when
Daddy brought my second hand smoking experience to an
abrupt end. Of course, he had good reason, as he was a very
wise man. The turning point came about one night following a basketball game. On this particular evening, one of
the star players, Bobby Joe Wells, had come home with me.
While Bobby Joe entertained Daddy with the highlights of
the game, I commenced to light Daddy's pipe for him. Next
thing I know, Daddy's shirt was on fire. You should have
seen me beating down the flames with one of Mama's sofa
pillows. It was a close call, and miraculously, his skin was not
burned. Seeing Daddy on fire was traumatic. I didn't have
to wait on triggers to remind me of that fiasco, for Bobby
Joe teased me every chance he got. One time he made me
so mad, I picked up a rock and aimed it at him. Bobby Joe
took off running with me chasing behind. It would take
years before I could look back and smile. Not so much at
Daddy's shirt being on fire, but at the image of Bobby Joe
running from me while I hurled a rock at his back.

Nearing the end of the school year, excitement was building around the senior prom. My biggest obstacle was transportation, especially since Sandra lived twenty miles away and I still had no car. As opposed to today when parents order those expensive limousines for their kids, there was nothing like that going on back in my day. The resolution to my transportation problem was solved when my friend, James Hambrick, another basketball star, and I decided to double date. James didn't have a car neither, but his dad, Deputy Sheriff Hambrick, was kind enough to loan him his Chevy which had one of those flashing lights on top. Imagine that!

I walked into the prom, arm in arm with Sandra. She was gorgeous in her gown and heels, and as far as the fellas go, I just knew I was the best dressed with a black tux that my Uncle Ferbee had sent me from Cleveland, Ohio.

Everything went fine with the evening and we delivered the girls safely back to their homes. Things, however, took a downward turn as we got closer to my home, and James made the turn on to Levine Street to drop me off. Within a few feet from my house, he suddenly lost focus and ran smack into a fire hydrant. We jumped out of the car to access the damage, a twelve inch dent on the right fender of his Dad's Chevy. For the longest time, James stood there with his mouth gaped open in shock. We'd had so much fun at the prom that I didn't want to ruin my evening or make him feel worse, so I tried to make light of the situation. "Man everything is going to be alright. Don't even worry about it." I turned and walked on into the house, glad that it wasn't me having to face his daddy.

▲ ▲ ▲

Mrs. Lomax, my homeroom teacher, was busy writing the agenda on the chalk board. Even though she was one of my favorite teachers, it had been difficult to keep my focus. I perked up when I noticed a recruitment presentation by the military scheduled for 10:00 a.m. in Mrs. Martin's class. Back then, all the seniors who chose the military headed off to the Army or Air Force. I never recalled anyone going into the Marine Corps.

At 10:00, Mrs. Martin had no trouble getting the students to settle down. Not only were the girls gawking at the airman with goo goo eyes, but the guys, including me, were inspired by the starched uniform and mirror-shiny boots. The airman represented a whole other world that I was anxious to see, and the seed of joining the military was planted in my mind that very day.

▲ ▲ ▲

In addition to the presentation by the military recruiter, Mrs. Lomax had arranged for a presentation by Pratt & Whitney Aircraft from Hartford, Connecticut. The recruiters offered full time employment with health care benefits and vacation days. This was definitely the best offer in town.

After talking it over with Terry Warren, we decided to pursue this opportunity together.

Mama and Daddy were also excited that this door of opportunity had opened for me, and for just a second, they exhaled a sigh of relief that I didn't have to follow in Daddy's footsteps, working in the mines.

▲ ▲ ▲

With the championship games and the prom behind me, I could finally experience the fullness of joy that all students live for. Graduation Day. Liberty's graduating class of 1966 was indeed small. Five years earlier, it had become noticeable that the school's population was dwindling. Turns out, the white school had begun recruiting some of our best athletes in order to improve their chances of winning. And, where the players went, the girls followed. Slowly but surely, more and more students began to leave Liberty. By the time I graduated in 1966, the graduation class was ten students strong. I can proudly boast that I was fourth in my entire class with a B minus average.

▲ ▲ ▲

A few days prior to graduation, I experienced an *I'll be damned* moment when I learned my legal first name was *Herman* and not *Jerry*. How the administrators at Liberty High found that out before I did made no sense to me. It was brought to my attention when Mrs. Lomax presented me with my graduation papers. "Who is this Herman guy?" I asked, baffled. "There's been some mistake! I'm the class president and the class clown. Everybody knows me. How can somebody mistake my name?"

Mrs. Lomax nodded her understanding as she too had been calling me, Jerry. "Not according to our records. We must go by your birth name, not your nick name."

Later, when I questioned Mama about it, she admitted that Daddy had made the decision to call me, Jerry. He wanted to name me after his grandfather, and that's the name they'd been calling me ever since they brought me home from the hospital as a baby.

Initially, I resisted embracing my true birth name. However, as time went on, I realized that I needed to accept *Herman* for legal and formal purposes where my birth certificate may be required to prove my identity. Aside from that, my closest friends and family refer to me as *Jerry, or Jericho,* thanks to my biological father, James Small, who added his own twist to the name, Jerry.

CHAPTER 4

ABOUT THREE WEEKS following my high school graduation, Mama prepared the best farewell dinner a young or even an old man could ever ask for. "Ain't no telling when you'll get a good home cooked meal again, so I want to send you off with some of your favorites - just to remember me by," Mama said smiling.

I planted a sloppy wet kiss on Mama's cheek. "Ain't no way I'm going to forget you, Mama. No way. And nobody in the whole state of West Virginia, can cook a better pot of collard greens and ham hocks than you."

I ate my final meal slow but heartily, barely saving room for the golden peach cobbler that Mama had just taken from the oven and placed on the counter to cool.

At Terry's house, his Mom had also prepared some of his favorite foods. There were tearful goodbyes at both houses and lots of prayers sent up asking the Lord to take care of us.

▲ ▲ ▲

On Friday, July 8, 1966, Terry and I boarded the Greyhound bus heading for Hartford, Connecticut. Boy were we excited! If either would dare to admit it, we were just a little nervous too. After all, it was our first time going away from home, hundreds of miles away from our family and friends.

Upon arrival to the big city, we checked in at the fabulous YMCA, located downtown on State Street. To get acquainted with our new surroundings, Terry and I took long walks and even boarded the public bus for a cross city tour of Hartford.

First thing Monday morning, we jumped out of bed to the sounds of the alarm clock, tired. We'd been too excited to sleep much the night before, but we were more excited to begin our first real job with Pratt & Whitney Aircraft.

The plan was to live at the YMCA until we had received two paychecks, after which we'd move to our very own apartment, just Terry and me, on our own for the first time in our young lives.

One of the most momentous events during that short stay at the 'Y' was meeting the famous basketball player, Bill Russell, who played center for the Boston Celtics. Mr. Russell lived close to the area and occasionally stopped by the 'Y' to shoot hoops with the fellas.

In my new position at Pratt & Whitney, I served as a bench mechanic, checking for burrs and faulty parts for aircraft engines and getting them ready for final assembly. I liked the job well enough, but it was the pay that excited me most. There was no paycheck to be cashed. At the end of the work week, the foreman would simply distribute an envelope with cash, along with a check stub summarizing our earnings and deductions. Holding my first wad of cash was exhilarating. I couldn't help but think of Daddy's payday back in the mines. There had been no, "Thank God it's payday-Friday" for him. No paycheck nor wad of cash did Daddy receive. Instead, the mine had a "company store" where the miners would go for all the food and supplies they needed in order to live. Many times, I had accompanied Mama to the company store where she loaded up as much as she could carry in her basket. No cash was ever exchanged. The items were simply noted in the books by the man who tended the store.

▲ ▲ ▲

Being in Hartford, more than 700 miles away, was a heck of a lot farther from Sandra than I realized. I was beginning to wonder how this long distance relationship was going to work. The first few days, I stood in a long line waiting to use one of the two payphones at the 'Y'. By the end of the second week, my phone calls to Sandra had dwindled. Just when I was beginning to accept that the relationship was about to fizzle out, I received a phone call. On the other end of the line was Sandra, in tears and babbling about her mother being upset. At first I didn't understand what she was going on about. "Calm down Sandra, and tell me what's going on," I urged.

Sandra stopped crying just long enough to tell me that she was pregnant. Then she started crying again. I was speechless. She then went on to explain her mother's reaction to the news that her 16 year old daughter was pregnant. And to boot, she'd never even met the father of her unborn grandchild. Sandra's mother had never been home during my visits, not even when I picked her up for the prom.

The news of Sandra's pregnancy was truly a bombshell. As my fear grew, my heart beat faster and louder. Sandra was extremely nervous about the baby she was carrying, and with me living so far away, she felt alone and I felt responsible. How I could remedy the situation was the question that haunted my dreams that night.

CHAPTER 5

──── ▲ ▲ ▲ ────

MAMA SAID I was too young and flat out refused to sign for me to get married. Terry didn't support the idea of marriage either, but what else would my sidekick say? We were still living at the 'Y,' saving up our money for our first apartment, and the adventures of life were just over the horizon. Our dreams had definitely not included a wife and a baby. Again, my thoughts returned to Daddy. Although he lacked a formal education, his work in the mines was extremely important to the industrial revolution of this country. Daddy was proud of that. He was also a man to be admired for he took care of his kids. All fifteen of them plus my sister, Alice, and me.

Surprisingly, it was Sandra's mother, whom I still hadn't met, who handled all the legalities for us to get married. She scheduled our blood tests and helped fill out the application for our marriage license. She even chose the preacher who by now was driving Sandra and me back to her house where our brief wedding ceremony was to be held. During the drive, we learned that Reverend Jones had never ever presided over a wedding before and ours would be his first.

While we were en route, Reverend Jones trailed behind a truck that had some pipes sticking out of its cab. Why the Reverend was having trouble gauging his distance, I cannot say, but the next thing I knew, the pipes from the truck came crashing right through the reverend's windshield, missing us by mere inches. What a calamity! Miraculously, no one was hurt. In a small town like ours, it didn't take long for the police to arrive. As still is the case today, the driver at fault is the driver in the rear. Needless to say, the officer issued the reverend a ticket and before too long we proceeded to Sandra's house where our brief wedding took place.

With absolutely no money forthcoming from either of our families, the result was a no-frills wedding. No cake cutting, no toasting, no first dance, not even a used wedding gown or tux for the bride and groom. Our guest list consisted of Uncle Alonzo from my side of the family and Auntie Brown from Sandra's side of the family. Mama didn't attend because she didn't want to leave Daddy alone. I can only speculate that Sandra's mother was still upset about her daughter being pregnant. Even though the wedding took place in the living room of her house, and she had arranged most of the details, my new mother-in-law never emerged from her room to share in our special day.

Immediately after repeating our vows to be husband and wife till death do we part, my new sixteen year old bride and I boarded the Greyhound. We were heading to

Bridgeport, Connecticut, where we planned to stay with my Uncle Carl and Aunt Emma.

▲ ▲ ▲

Due to work obligations at Pratt & Whitney, Terry had remained in Bridgeport and was unable to attend my wedding. When I stopped by the 'Y' to collect my belongings, he muttered, "Congratulations." The sentiment, however, didn't quite show in his eyes. Indeed, we'd had a rude awakening from our dreams, and I understood how he felt. On the flip side, I felt good that I had done the right thing by marrying Sandra. It would be years before I'd see Terry again.

▲ ▲ ▲

I was truly grateful for Uncle Carl and Aunt Emma who provided Sandra and me with room and board. To help get us on our feet as fast as possible, I took on two jobs, working practically day and night. First, at Fagins restaurant, I stood for long hours washing dishes and cleaning up the small Italian restaurant. When Mr. Fagin asked me how I was coming along, my only complaint was that my feet ached. With a dismissive wave of his hand, he said, "Oh, you'll get used to it."

My second place of employment was Bill's Furniture Upholstery Store. The owner, Mr. Bill, spent hours teaching me how to sew together various fabrics. I really enjoyed this new trade a whole lot more than the restaurant.

Unfortunately, on the homefront, Sandra was growing bored and lonely. She was also homesick and missed her mother and sisters. I didn't have a chance to see her during the day, for the long bus ride between one job and the next left no time for me to go home. Thus, she was left alone for far too many hours.

It didn't take too long for us to succumb to the pressures of married life and young parents-to-be. Time has faded most of the memories that caused friction between my young bride and me. I do, however, recall one occasion when I asked Sandra if she could fix me something to eat. I'd arrived home late, tired after working both of my jobs, and I was famished.

Sandra was so sweet when she answered, "of course."

When I raised the spoon to my mouth, I was imagining I was back in Williamson, seated at Mama's table in her kitchen. With my mouth salivating, I bit into the chicken pot pie that Sandra had lovingly baked in the oven and placed before me. To my dismay, I bit straight into a frozen mass of vegetables. Trying my best to hide my disappointment, I continued to chew every little frozen crystal. Before taking another bite, I poked around the small pot pie with my spoon searching for an area soft and well done. Sandra had good intentions, but unfortunately, there were sprinkles of frozen ice through and through.

I was eighteen and Sandra was sixteen. Mama had the wisdom when she forewarned me that I was too young to get married. However, I had to grow into that understanding through my own experience.

After quitting both of my jobs, Sandra and I boarded the Greyhound and returned to Williamson where we stayed with Mama for a couple of months. I could only hope that while we were there, Sandra would learn her way around the kitchen, if only half as good as Mama.

CHAPTER 6

▲ ▲ ▲

GOOD PAYING JOBS in Williamson were hard to find, especially making enough to support a wife and new baby. Therefore, it wasn't hard for my friend Ronald Blackwell to convince me to accompany him to the recruiting office of the United States Marine Corps. At that time, there was a program known as "The Buddy Plan." The recruiter did an excellent job at explaining all the benefits of serving our country, along with the salary and opportunities for education/ training after being discharged. I had heard it all before from the recruiter who came to Liberty High, so I was ready. I felt the Marine Corps might finally provide me with some direction for my life.

So far I had only ridden the Greyhound bus, back and forth from West Virginia, to Connecticut, six times. Not exactly the plan that Terry and I had mapped out since graduating from high school, four months earlier. I was desperate for a positive change. Plus, the military would offer the financial benefits that would help me support my wife and our baby who was just starting to move in Sandra's womb.

After talking it over with Mama, we all thought it would be a good idea for Sandra to remain with her. After all,

Mama had raised enough children and had the experience to help Sandra, especially during a time when she and her own mother were not on the best terms.

▲ ▲ ▲

On October 10, 1966, Ronald and I boarded the Greyhound bus to Charleston, South Carolina. From Charleston, we boarded a military bus headed for Parris Island. The ride was about four hours, and every time I tried to nod off, the image of Sandra's tearful goodbyes invaded my thoughts. Between quivering lips, she had made me promise to come back. It had been a bittersweet farewell for me. While I was excited about my future with the Marine Corps, I hated leaving my pregnant wife behind.

When Ronald and I arrived at Parris Island, tired and hungry, we were greeted by a welcome committee of one angry drill instructor who yelled out, "Hurry up and get the fuck off this bus, you maggots." My imaginary image of Parris Island with palm trees and white sandy beaches suddenly vanished.

Shortly after our "friendly" welcome, Ronald and I stood in a line with the other recruits awaiting our turn in the barber's chair. Hippies sat down and within three seconds flat, their long hair lay in heaps on the floor. I actually saw tears in the eyes of one recruit as he stared regretfully at his hair on the floor. As I continued to watch and the bleeding scalps continued to increase, I began to mentally rehearse how I'd ask the barber to change the blade and not cut mine so close. But, by the time I sat down in his chair, I must have grown some alligator skin, for somehow I'd found the discipline to keep my lips sealed, just like all the others before me. For my reward, I escaped the bleeding scalp syndrome.

Finally, after the mundane three second buzz cuts, shots, and physicals, Ronald and I were issued our 782 gear and weapon, an M14 rifle.

Ronald and I were assigned to 2nd Battalion, Platoon 304. Unfortunately, during some of the strenuous training, he sustained a knee injury and was removed from our platoon. The next time I saw him was in a chow hall many months later in the Philippines.

At Parris Island, which has been the site for marine recruit training since 1815, I learned how to survive in a stressful environment with little sleep and little food. Bootcamp was rigorous, and my training officers were relentless. Still, I was filled with excitement and adventure.

CHAPTER 7

$$\blacktriangle \, \blacktriangle \, \blacktriangle$$

In early November, 1966, I was "snapping in" on the rifle range when I was approached by my command officer with some news from home. "Williams, step in my office," he said. "Have you been writing home?"

"Yes, sir. I have."

"Well, I want to tell you something. Things happen in life. Things that are out of our control. We just received word that your grandfather has died. I'm sending you to get fitted for your uniform and you're on emergency leave."

My grandfather, Daddy, had suffered a stroke and died. I was shocked. I knew he wasn't in the best of health, but I wasn't expecting him to die. I hated that I'd never get to see the pride in his eyes seeing me in my Marine Corps uniform for the first time. He'd been proud of all his sons who went into the military. I also hated that Daddy would never see my first born. I had mentally rehearsed the moment I'd introduce him to my own child and how I would let him know how much he had inspired me to be a father. I could only pray that I'd be half as good a daddy as he had been.

During boot camp, I wore the utility greens which consisted of green pants, green shirt and a green hat. But, for

Daddy's funeral, I was allowed to wear my new dress greens uniform. My uniform definitely made a statement and the comment, "You sure look good in your uniform," was mentioned several times at the funeral. I didn't want it to be known that I was blushing, but I had to admit, they were telling the truth.

I'm not exactly sure why Sandra did not attend, but I recall feeling that a wife should be by her husband's side at a time like this. Daddy's death was my first encounter with death of a loved one, and it was heartbreaking, especially when Mama cried out.

▲ ▲ ▲

Seven days after Daddy was laid to rest, I returned to boot camp. Since the week out for attending his funeral had placed me too far behind my original platoon, I would have to spend additional time in boot camp. I was therefore reassigned. I didn't consider it a problem. In my mind, additional training could only make me a better marine. Although I returned to boot camp with a positive frame of mind, my welcome was anything but. Still in my uniform, the new drill instructor called me out. "You maggot, I'll give you ten seconds to take off my uniform." Before I could unbuckle my pants, he yelled, again. "Give me one thousand push-ups." Immediately I dropped to the ground, conscious not to show my humiliation, especially in front of the new trainees who had less experience than I had. *One thousand push-ups? Is he crazy?* I thought. But crazy or not,

I began popping them off, 1-2-3... Fortunately, the drill instructor had the good sense to stop me when I got close to fifty.

Many times during the remainder of my training, the drill instructor called me out. Eventually, I learned that he was really trying to showcase me as an example to the new guys, and at the same time, he was molding me into a better marine.

During Fire Watch Training, on a rotating basis every two hours, one trainee had to remain awake on watch in the squad bay while the others slept in their bunks. The assigned trainee would walk up and down the aisle making sure everything was alright. No one could get up in the middle of the night, no talking and no movement. The training was designed to mold us to listen intently and watch for the enemy, while in the field.

My drill instructor also taught me, the hard way, all about my weapon. On the outside of the military, guns were guns. But not in the military. "Never call this a gun," he'd said, holding a rifle in his hands. "You may call it a rifle, if it's a rifle, but basically, this is your weapon. And, until you've proved yourself worthy by making it through boot camp, this is *my* weapon."

As a young recruit, unaccustomed to carrying any weight at all on my back, I found my weapon, combined with my 782 gear, heavy and awkward, especially when carrying them some distance. With about 60 pounds on our backs, we were ordered to go across a sand pit that seemed like a half mile from the barracks.

One day while carrying my heavy sea bag, my weapon fell off my back and dropped in the sand. Within an instant, the drill instructor was spit shouting in my face. "You fucking maggot. Pick up my weapon! When we get to the barracks, I'm going to work the shit out of you!" Then as if to show his anger even more, he stepped closer and punctuated each syllable. "You are going to clean every speck of dirt from my weapon!" True to his word, I was one of the first ones he ordered to drop and give him 100 push-ups. Afterwards, I took particular care in cleaning every speck of sand and dirt from my/his weapon.

Over the next few weeks, we carried sand buckets filled to the brim with sand to build up our muscles. In contrast to the scrawny kid I'd been prior to joining the Marine Corps, I soon became muscle bound and in terrific shape. By the time I completed boot camp, I had learned to carry all my equipment, without dropping it, and even managed to tread water with all my equipment on my back.

I became a "marine" after graduating from boot camp. No more fucking maggots, pigs, or any of the other derogatory names that our drill sergeants invariably called us. After graduation, "his" weapon became "my" weapon.

CHAPTER 8

▲ ▲ ▲

IN MID-JANUARY, 1967, following boot camp, I was sent to Camp Lejeune, in Jacksonville, North Carolina. For six weeks, I would undergo Infantry Training Regiment (ITR), where I learned the following life sustaining skills:

- Discipline
- Hand to hand combat
- Survival training
- How to operate every weapon in the Marine Corps arsenal
- Never leave a fellow marine behind, dead or wounded
- Never underestimate the enemy
- Nothing is impossible. If you can crawl, you can walk. If you can walk, you can run. There is no such thing as can't.

The discipline training I received was really significant. In fact, it corrected my short temper that had landed me in plenty of fights during my youth. I learned when one is provoked to anger, it's hard to perform – you can't think clearly. I can truly attest that the Marine Corps corrected this uncontrollable anger in me. In the days ahead, I would come to see it tried and tested, and I would forever have Staff Sergeant Pelligreeni to thank.

During one of the training exercises, Pelligreeni went into a facility and left the squad outside at parade rest. If we were standing right there and another person outside our unit tried to go through our lines, the entire unit was supposed to react. "Don't let nobody break your rank, or interrupt your flow," was the rule that Pelligreeni drilled into us. Then to make sure we had learned our lesson, he set us up by having another marine, unknown to us, walk through our line. The entire squad did what was expected - our entire platoon, on top of one intruder. We really could have hurt him, but when Pelligreeni commanded, "At ease," we immediately ceased our aggression. This component of our discipline training taught us how to care for each other.

During another exercise, hand to hand combat, Sergeant Pelligreeni forced me to slap another recruit in the face. I obeyed, but lacking an inclination to really hurt my fellow trainee, I didn't slap him as hard as I could have. "Harder!" Sergeant Pelligreeni growled. "He was talking about your daddy." As a youngster, I'd been pretty good at playing "the dozens," and talking smack about my daddy was indeed fighting words. Suddenly, my anger kicked in and pow! I hit my fellow recruit as hard as I could. Needless to say, he retaliated and the fight was on.

For another hand to hand technique, we were provided pogo sticks, padded on each end, simulating a bayonet. Learning this skill would be a survival option, just in case we ran out of ammunition for our weapon.

Rifle range training was a real disappointment to my ego. I had been diligent in practice and wanted desperately to prove my sergeant wrong. "I'm going to tell you something right now, maggot. You are *not* going to qualify!" he had bellowed in my face. In spite of all my efforts, I could not prove him wrong. Because I failed to make one minor adjustment, I missed becoming an expert shooter by a mere two points. In the end, I finished as a sharp shooter, which was still very good, but one level less than my own personal goal.

We were also trained to carry deadweight which I found amazing. In no time at all, I was able to distribute a recruit's weight, over 200 pounds, haul him over my shoulders and carry him with minimal strain. I also learned to run while carrying a recruit over my shoulder.

Gas Chamber Training was a painfully, tormenting experience. For this exercise, my fellow recruits and I were seated in the bleachers of a big building in a hangar, listening to an officer lecture about tear gas. For a real life experience, other officers were sneaking around behind us, busting tear gas canisters. Within seconds, our eyes began to overflow with tears. Involuntarily, we all sprang up from our seats running in various directions, covering our eyes.

After clearing our eyes of all the tears, my fellow recruits and I were ushered inside another big building called the gas chamber. After the entire crew crammed inside, the door slammed shut. As the gas filled the air, our skin began to burn followed by uncontrollable coughing and choking.

Gas had also seeped up our nostrils causing snot to come streaming down.

Outside of the building, several marines were holding the door closed. My fellow recruits and I pushed on the door, and we beat on the door, calling out to our saviors. For some that was mama, for others that was God. Eventually, one recruit managed to squeeze his hand through the door. With the rest of us as reinforcement, we were able to push through. We ran for the hills gasping for fresh air. A few of the trainees were also selected to take a shot from a needle to neutralize the effects of the gas. The Marine Corps was certainly getting us ready for any and every type of combat weaponry, whether it was likely we'd experience it or not.

Gas chamber training was one rare occasion when the command officer didn't yell at us or make us endure any additional consequences. I guess the tear gas had been torture enough. This intensive training was also designed to weed out those recruits who really didn't have the fortitude to go the distance. In the Marine Corps, only the strong survive. I bought into the training, hook, line and sinker. I wanted to be the best I could be and once I finished, it was my desire to return to Williamson and stand before the Liberty High senior class as a marine, the first marine. As far as I knew, most of the seniors who left to join the military joined the Army, Air Force or Navy. I didn't know anyone who had joined the Marine Corps, and I wanted to be the first. I wanted the teachers and students to be as proud of me as I'd been of the military soldiers who had come during my senior year seeking new recruits.

CHAPTER 9

▲ ▲ ▲

ON MARCH 6, 1967, while still in Infantry Training (ITR) in Lejeune, North Carolina, I awoke from a deep sleep, feeling ill. It happened suddenly. The pain in my stomach was severe, nothing like I'd ever experienced before. When I went to see the corpsman, I was immediately placed in quarantine. Little did I know that back in the states, Sandra had gone into labor. Hours later, while lying on my sick bed, scared of the unknown, one of the doctors rushed in with a big grin on his face. "Good news, marine. Your blood work shows no problems, and your wife just had a baby girl." Immediately I sat up in bed and miraculously began to feel better. It was like I had gone through labor with Sandra, across thousands of miles, like mental telepathy. It was an amazing experience. Truly phenomenal!

It was weeks later, while on a ten day leave, that I first laid eyes on my sweet baby girl. Once again, I traveled to Williamson by Greyhound. This time, Sandra was at the station to meet me. In her arms, was our sweet baby girl. She was so small and immediately, my heart swelled with much love. When I touched her tiny finger, she grabbed hold, like she knew I was her Daddy. It pleased me to no end that Sandra allowed me to name our daughter "Francine," after a beautiful actress who I knew only from a movie.

The ten day visit with Mama, my baby and my wife was the calm before the storm. My orders had come, and as soon as I returned to the base, I would be shipped out to Camp Pendleton in California for four weeks of jungle warfare training. From there, I would be sent off to war. The Vietnam War.

During the early part of April, 1967, I headed to Camp Pendleton, California, to begin more rigorous training. The focus this time was jungle warfare. Twelve years had already passed since the Vietnam War had begun and training was updated regularly to simulate the actual villages, buildings and fox holes that we would encounter in the bush.

To stimulate our psyche in preparation for battle in Vietnam, we watched old combat videos that depicted the enemy at their best, not to be taken for granted. I recall being amazed that 100 years earlier, the enemy had dug into the ground and made reinforced concrete bunkers. Although we learned that the old bunkers were still there, we would be digging new ones, as it was feared that the old bunkers were subjected to all types of booby traps.

In terms of our weapons, the new M16s were just being introduced. "These are new fully automatic weapons, made by Mattel, and they are swell," the instructor announced. To demonstrate, the instructor placed the stock (the butt) of the M16 under his chin and pulled the trigger. The automatic burst rapidly fired multiple rounds, but his hand barely moved. Indeed it was lightweight, as compared to the M-14 we had previously trained with during boot camp. A lighter weapon was definitely needed during jungle warfare, considering all the other equipment we'd need to tote around.

CHAPTER 10

— ▲ ▲ ▲ —

ON MAY 30, 1967, our unit boarded a commercial plane from Camp Pendleton en route to Hawaii. From Hawaii, we boarded another commercial plane heading to Okinawa, Japan. After a brief layover at the Kadena Air Force Base, we boarded a huge Gov Air, C-130 military plane. This would be our final flight heading directly to Da Nang, Vietnam. Just before take-off, steam began to fill-up in the compartment. Within minutes, it was discovered that the plane had engine problems and the take-off was aborted. Had I been a civilian passenger on a commercial plane, this breakdown may have caused me some anxiety. However, being in the Marine Corps, I had no doubts that the problem would be taken care of expeditiously. I did, however, stop and offer thanks to my guardian angel, that the problem was detected while we were still on the runway.

Within a couple of hours, we were transferred to another C-130 which took us uneventfully from Okinawa, to Da Nang, Vietnam. As the plane glided through the sky, I tried to relax, relieved and proud of the fact that I had successfully made it through nine strenuous weeks of boot camp, six weeks of grueling infantry training, followed by another four weeks of special jungle training. Now, it was time to put my skills to the real test. I was pumped full of confidence and ready to serve my country as a soldier in the United States Marine Corps.

The Vietnam War was also known as the Second Indochina War, and known in Vietnam as Resistance War Against America. The official date that the Americans got involved in the Vietnam War was November 1, 1955. The war ended early in May, 1975. According to the statistics found on History-World.org., more than 9,000,000 military personnel served during the Vietnam era. Twenty-five percent were drafted, but I was one of thousands who voluntarily enlisted. Servicemen in the army served twelve months in country per tour of duty. Marines, however, served an additional month of duty, totaling thirteen months. My personal contributions to the Vietnam War began in June, 1967. At that time, I was ranked as Private First Class, Herman L. Williams.

On June 4, 1967, the Gov Air military plane landed at the airbase in Da Nang, Republic of Vietnam (RVN). Young Vietnamese girls were running around in black pjs and straw hats selling sodas to the hordes of American soldiers standing around with weapons in hand. Other vendors were selling all kinds of food and souvenirs. Planes roared above. What a rare sight!

My fellow marines and I soon realized that although we had trained together, we would not fight in the war together. Psychologically, this separation was for our benefit, as we would have fewer emotional ties to unfamiliar marines, therefore fewer distractions in the thick of the war zone. "Williams, you're going up north. You'll be assigned to Unit 2/4," announced the staff sergeant.

Little did I know that Unit 2/4, or 2nd Battalion, 4th Marines, was one of the most prestigious units in the history of the U.S. Marines. Unit 2/4 was constituted in 1914, during World War I, and activated as one of the three battalions of the 4th Marine Regiment. Historically, Unit 2/4 has fought valiantly to bring an end to numerous assaults, stateside and abroad, including conflicts in the Dominican Republic, China, Corregidor, Vietnam, Iraq and Afghanistan.

The coat of arms was designed in 1964, by Lt. Colonel Doxey and his wife. It was modified later in 1965, by Lt. Colonel Fisher to include the words, "The Magnificent Bastards." This nickname became official by Battalion Order 5600.1B in September, 1966, during the Vietnam War. Pictured below, the insignia's crest is scarlet and gold representing the dress and display colors of the Marine Corps. The blue background represents soldiers of the sea, the seahorse is representative of our amphibious nature, the palm trees represent our duty in the Caribbean, Hawaii, and the torri represents our tours of duty in the Far East.

History of coat of arms is referenced at
http://www.2-4association.org/files/2-4_CoatArms.pdf

▲ ▲ ▲

A convoy of sixbye (military trucks) left Da Nang Air Base heading north on Highway 1, to the Second Battalion, Fourth Marines, (Unit 2/4). I had expected to arrive at my battalion and have a little time to settle in. Little did I know that the action would be imminent. Along the way, a couple sixbye trucks in the convoy were blown up from mines buried on Highway 1. Fresh in country, within a few hours of landing in Vietnam, a number of marines became instant casualties.

▲ ▲ ▲

During my former weeks of training, there'd been very few black marines to be seen. I was taken aback when I arrived in Unit 2/4 and found that the majority of the marines in the platoon I was assigned to were black. These marines also held positions that I never thought I'd see occupied by a black men. Some had rank like the machine gunner and rocket marine, who had a tremendous number of kills. I was proud of them and proud to become a marine in that unit, also known as the Magnificent Bastards.

I was assigned to the first platoon which consisted of four squads, with 12 men in each squad. The platoon commander also appointed me to serve as a fire team leader, with six marines under my command including a machine gunner, rifleman, a radio man, an M-79 rocket launcher, a point man and infantry man, also known as a grunt.

Being in Unit 2/4 meant we had no base camp of our own. We would be on the move constantly from one village to another, on ambushes (day and night), making routine patrols on foot, carrying out search and destroy missions, and blocking forces. When each operation or mission was complete, those soldiers who were fortunate enough to make it back alive would simply enter through the rear of the closest base camp in our particular locale. These marine base camps were located at various points along Highway 1, which stretched from North Vietnam to South Vietnam.

▲ ▲ ▲

For a war that would last as long as twenty years, a mere thirteen months did not appear too lengthy for one soldier, or so I first thought. However, I would come to experience complications in terms of the climate, too extreme to accurately describe. First of all, the heat in itself was an assault with average temperatures exceeding 120 degrees, in the shade. Then there was the monsoon season when it rained countless days and nights. With no shelter to escape to for days on end, combined with the weight of my uniform and equipment, needless to say, I was either soaked from the sweltering heat or soaked from the rain, both day and night.

For thirteen months, if we were fortunate to still be alive, we would live in the bush, sleep little, eat little food, other than some wild bananas and C-rations. Thirteen months suddenly seemed too far away to count or look forward to.

▲ ▲ ▲

I can honestly say that during my tour in Vietnam, I had very little knowledge of the territory that I covered or how many operations or missions I participated in. However, one of the most significant was my very first combat mission, which took place on my second night in Vietnam. To the best that my recollection can surmise, in conjunction with details from my military records, Operation Choctaw was underway. Our location for the all-night ambush was near Thua Thien Province, Republic of Vietnam (RVN). Thua Thien Province is located in South Vietnam.

At 2100 hours, I set out on foot with three others: Our fire team leader, Sergeant Queen; two other marines; and myself, the FNG, short for 'fucking new guy.' I was geared up with my helmet, flight jacket, jungle utility pants, and jungle boots which contained a special plate in the bottom to prevent penetration of sharp objects that would be used as booby traps. We never wore gloves - our bare hands were always exposed. The consequences of which I still struggle with today. On a daily basis I deal with seriously dry and rough hands by applying a medicated ointment provided by the VA.

Our squad of four walked approximately two miles, or in military terms, 3218.6 meters from the compound which was located near Camp Evans, a former U.S. Army and Marine Corps base located west of Highway 1. The camp was named after Marine Lance Corporal Paul Evans who was killed during Operation Chinook, in 1966. We traveled light, leaving our 782 gear backpacks behind. Of course I carried my M16 and magazines, my cartridge belt, my bayonet, my grenade pouch with grenades and two water canteens.

When we reached our ambush location, Sergeant Queen ordered us to stop and get into our prone position, down in the bamboo grass or what we called elephant grass which stood about neck high. The sky was our blanket and the moon was our light. Back in the states, the night air, even in July, would have cooled things off a bit. Not the case in Vietnam, where the extreme heat and humidity measured in temperatures over 120 degrees.

Each of us was assigned watch duty, alternating in spans of two hours while the other three marines slept. Should we notice any sign of the enemy, we were to tap the other's right boot, by the big toe. We were just that disciplined to wake up at such a moment.

Lying in the thickness of the bamboo grass, I listened intently and watched for the enemy. When it was my turn to get some shut-eye, I couldn't sleep a wink. I didn't want to miss a thing. I was constantly checking the time on my watch and my sergeant's watch too. I listened, straining to recognize the strange sounds to which nothing similar had been introduced during training. Out in the bush of Vietnam were water buffaloes; poisonous bamboo snakes, (mister two step - take one step and the next you're dead); treacherous leeches and mosquitoes which we had learned during training not to even blow or swat at. The unfamiliar sounds certainly had my mind racing and my adrenaline pumping.

I remember being amazed at the knot of fear growing in my stomach, and the thoughts that were quickly filling my head. *How could I feel this nervous after so much preparation? How was I going to feel when I made my first kill? Was the enemy really coming? Was this a trick?* Knowing full well I was in the real theater of Vietnam, I had no choice but to sum it all up. In spite of all my diligent training and mental preparation, when it got right down to it, I was s-c-a-r-e-d. The excitement of combat was fading fast, along with my patriotic zeal. My reality check was fully activated. Words can't even describe the relief I felt when the first ambush ended with absolutely no contact by the enemy.

▲ ▲ ▲

Following our first night ambush, we returned to the rear camp where the officers were waiting for us. The acute fear soon vanished and my confidence returned. The platoon commander explained our next mission, and the anticipated number of casualties. He reiterated that life expectancy for Unit 2/4 was a mere thirty seconds during the Vietnam War.

Since I was the new guy, Sergeant Queen issued my first direct assignment. "Williams, I need you to disassemble the claymore mine." We had set the claymore mine out in front of our ambush position. If the enemy got close, one click on the plunger would trigger off the blasting cap. At least twenty would have been killed with a single blast.

"Yes, sir," I replied and began the task. I pulled the blasting cap from the claymore mine and proceeded to pull the mine out of the mud. Foolishly, I left out one very important step in the process. Inadvertently, I mashed the plunger and the damn thing went off. Rookie mistake. Everyone hit the deck as mud flew everywhere. "Sergeant Queen, you'd better watch that fng," the lieutenant growled with a scowl. "He's going to get us all killed!"

Sometimes it takes years to be able to laugh at a serious situation, as now is the case, almost fifty years later. Today, I'm shaking my head at the vision of those soldiers running scared, not knowing it was only mud sailing through the air, but fearing it was fragments of shrapnel, aiming to kill 'em. Hilarious.

Sergeant Queen later reported to the lieutenant that I was an *alright* marine, alert during the entire ambush, and never slept a wink.

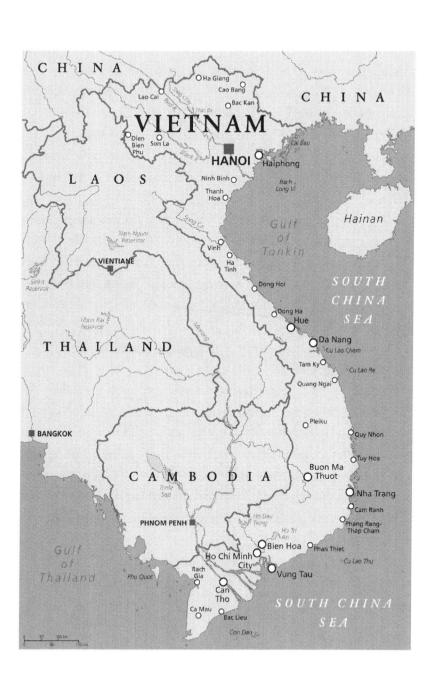

CHAPTER 11

— ▲ ▲ ▲ —

WE BARELY HAD time to debrief my first night ambush before we received orders for the next mission, a day time ambush. Unfortunately, we would not return to base camp and report no enemy contact, as several fellow marines were shot by North Vietnamese Army snipers. We, the marines, were supporting South Vietnam.

▲ ▲ ▲

Before and after every operation or mission, Unit 2/4 would come in through the rear gate of the nearest marine base camp. These base camps were located near the cities of Phu Bai; Hue; Dong Ha; Con Thien; and Khe Sanh. The commander of the base camp would alert the other marines within the camp that Unit 2/4 will be coming through. During these short breaks from action in the bush, they'd show us much respect and hospitality.

Marine base camps were located at various points along Highway 1, which stretches from North Vietnam to South Vietnam. The Con Thien base was located as far north as you can go, near the demilitarized zone (DMZ), an area where neither the Americans, nor the Vietnamese were supposed to occupy. It was a neutral zone, close to the border of North Vietnam. While the other camps were above ground, the Con Thien base was located underground, surrounded with barbed wire and mines planted along its perimeter to help protect the base from the NVA. Supplies had to be dropped from helicopters. From time to time, various works of art could be seen on the bottom of helicopters flying above us – including an image of a middle finger meant for the enemy lurking around. With all the drama we were going through, we enjoyed this bit of humor.

Another base camp was located near the City of Hue. I was simply awestruck with the beauty of Hue's Colonial French architecture. Its Catholic schools and churches were far more magnificent than any school or church I've ever seen. Many of the structures throughout Hue were built by the French over 100 years earlier. Before too long, I would live to see this beautiful city destroyed.

CHAPTER 12

———————— ▲ ▲ ▲ ————————

On July 20, 1967, I turned 20 years old. I had only been in Vietnam one month, and with so many soldiers losing their lives around me, it seemed rather trivial for me to be celebrating. Therefore, I made no mention of it. I could only pray I would make it out of Vietnam alive and that this birthday would not be my last.

I would also have to say it was truly peculiar that on my birthday I tried to save a life, but fate took it instead. My fire team had been resting at the base of a rice paddy, below Highway 1. We were cleaning our weapons and preparing for an upcoming night ambush near a village on the other side of Highway 1. Operation Fremont was underway and we were in position near Thua Thien Province. Suddenly, we were fired upon, and for about ten minutes, we exchanged fire with the enemy. As we assaulted the hill to evaluate the damage, dead bodies were sprawled on the ground and a Vietnamese home, (hooch) was engulfed in flames. I'm not sure if our unit was responsible, but with temperatures above 100 degrees and a hooch made of straw, it wouldn't take much nor would it take long to burn to the ground. A young Vietnamese mother was pointing to the flames and screaming, "em be cua toi; em be cua toi," meaning, "my baby, my baby." I didn't speak the Vietnamese language, so an interpreter relayed the mother's plea. Even had there been no interpreter, I would have understood, judging from her panic stricken face. Quickly, I lowered my equipment from my back and handed it to a fellow marine. I then rushed inside the burning hooch. Smoke was intense, so I dropped to the floor and crawled around, listening intently for the cries of a baby in distress. Upon locating the baby, I grabbed it and began backing away from the flames licking at my hands. Outside the hooch, in the broad daylight, I realized the full scope of the baby's demise. Smoke was rising from the small body which was scorched to a crisp. As if to snap me out of any psychological tension that might overwhelm me at that moment, my lieutenant yelled out. "Williams, drop that baby and let's get out of here!"

The baby was hot and my hands felt as if they were melting into its skin. As I handed the charred baby into the mother's outstretched hands, she dropped to her knees clutching it to her breast. The agonizing scream that escaped from her lips trailed behind me for what seemed like miles.

For days, I would find myself shaking my hands as if to purge the heat that continued to linger on the tips of my fingers. If I were not a victim of PTSD, my damaged nerves in itself would be a constant reminder. However, in relation to PTSD is a compulsive behavior whereby I wash my hands over and over with extremely hot water. One therapist suggested that I'm washing stains from the dead baby. Even after forty years, the VA still supplies me with ointment for my hands.

Due to PTSD, the tragedy of the little baby would later become one of my worst nightmares, complete with the scent of burning flesh and smoke.

CHAPTER 13

▲ ▲ ▲

MY FIRST KILL occurred during the early part of September, 1967. Around this time, Operation Liberty was underway and we were set up in the area of Phu Bai. I was out in the flank in an area where NVA snipers had been detected. Had I not spotted the enemy about forty feet away, he would have taken out the entire spine of our squad. Unfortunately for him, he did not notice me.

I cannot fully explain the feeling knowing that I was about to make my first kill, but I do recall a tightness in my gut that I had never experienced before. With my selector set on fully automatic, I opened up my M16 weapon and a burst of gunfire followed. The bullets went straight through the enemy's neck, killing him instantly. The other two who were with him took off running, disappearing into the bush. Keeping my aim in their direction, I pulled the trigger again. Instead of the burst of automatic gunfire that I was expecting, my weapon was silent. Not even a click. I was thoroughly bewildered as it registered that my weapon had suddenly jammed. Sergeant Queen suddenly appeared at my side. "Williams, you did a good job."

"It all happened so fast, sir. I was expecting to spray all three of them. I got one, but the other two ran and got away because of this friggin M16. This damn thing jammed. Made by Mattel, designed to swell, my ass," I protested. "This was my first kill. When we need them most, during hostile fire, they ain't so reliable, huh?"

Sergeant Queen shook his head indicating that he understood. Later, in an effort to minimize future jamming, we used our C-rations, mainly franks and beans, to lubricate the M16.

CHAPTER 14

——————— ▲ ▲ ▲ ———————

BECAUSE OF MY ability to perform without hesitating during my first kill, it was decided that I should learn to "Walk Point." Walking point is the point person, first to go in on a patrol or mission. Whatever is discovered upon entry is then relayed to the marines coming up from the rear. It was Lance Corporal Valdez who took me under his wing. "A lot of people are afraid to walk point. But, I'm going to teach you all you need to know," he'd said. Valdez was a full blooded Puerto Rican from New York with lots of jokes. Months later, I was a firsthand eye witness to a crucial mistake that he'd make following an explosion in the bush. The demolition man had cleared an area for a medevac chopper to land. He had wired up some bamboo poles to clear the area. Once he set up the explosion, we were taught to stay down until he yelled, "Fire in the hole." If you raise up too fast, you risk debris flying in your face. In spite of his excellent teachings, Valdez, himself, made that very crucial mistake. We were out in the bush when he screamed out. "Aww, a piece of bamboo done messed up a million dollar face like mine." How he could spit out such humor following such a disaster still has me chuckling to this day.

Unfortunately, the bamboo left a nasty mark on Valdez's forehead, a permanent reminder of the Vietnam War.

Valdez was also instrumental in reinforcing my discipline to keep cool when faced with a sticky situation. Such an occasion presented itself shortly after I found my friend, Joe, killed and mutilated with his own government-issued, entrenching tool, (e-tool.) Joe's repulsive death temporarily prejudiced me towards *all* Vietnamese. The first one I saw back at the base camp took the brunt of my anger. All I could think of was revenge. With no forethought, I went up to the Vietnamese, an Army Republic of Vietnam (ARVIN) South Vietnamese soldier, one of the ones we were there to protect, and struck him with the butt of my weapon. Before things could escalate, Valdez stepped in. "Calm it down, marine. Keep it cool. Don't let it get to you. He is not the enemy. I know Joe was your boy, but you can't let it get to you."

▲ ▲ ▲

Around mid-September, the heavens opened up and poured out rain, day and night. This rainy season, known as the monsoon season, lasted several months. During monsoon season, we struggled to stay on higher ground. During previous wars, the French had dug reinforced concrete bunkers that would fill up with water. The enemy, who knew the whereabouts of these bunkers, camouflaged their entry with bamboo. Consequently, many marines fell in. Some drowned, and those dead soaked bodies had to be hauled on our backs to a designated place where they were lifted into helicopters. Still there were other marines whose bodies were lost, never to be recovered.

During training, we'd been taught to take care of our feet by changing our socks often to keep our feet dry. This of course was next to impossible during the monsoon season. There were times when I stood waste deep in standing water while heavy rain poured over my body from above.

▲ ▲ ▲

On another patrol, I was walking along a river bank when snipers opened up. With shrapnel flying all around, I dove over a hedgerow, or so I thought. To my horror and surprise, it turned out to be a river. Deep down into the water, I shed all of my 782 gear and began to swim upwards. The water was so murky I could barely see mere inches above me. All the while I was thinking, *what a hell of a way to go.* That was the only occasion that I was glad for the scorching temperatures, as a frozen river would truly have complicated my swimming ability. As I continued to swim upward, my legs began to tire. I remember thinking, *I can't drink all this damn water,* when suddenly, I felt a pull under my chin. Right in the nick of time, I was lifted upwards. I had made it to within two feet of shallow water when one of my fellow marines pulled me to safety where I could start breathing on my own. Out of breath, I managed a grateful nod to my fellow marine whose name I cannot remember.

CHAPTER 15

WITHIN THREE SHORT months after my arrival in Vietnam, I made rank from a Private First Class (PFC) to a Lance Corporal. Getting rank that fast was an amazing feat, especially for a black man at age nineteen. Normally, marines promoted to this rank had to show leadership and skill in serving as a role model. The happenstance of this scenario presented me with the opportunity, because I just happened to be in the right place at the right time.

After the mandatory thirteen month tour of duty ended for the other marines in my unit and they were shipped out, I just happened to be the only marine left in my unit. As the new marines arrived, they naturally looked up to me. Casualties were stacking up and so far, I was still amongst the living. The new fngs were anxious to learn all they could to stay alive, and I had no problem stepping up to provide assistance in whatever way I could. It didn't matter that I'd only been in Vietnam for three short months, I still had that many more months experience than they had. I was later informed that my display of leadership warranted my promotion to Lance Corporal.

Shortly after I made Lance Corporal, my platoon commander approached me and explained that he had submitted a request for me to take one week out of Vietnam for rest and recuperation, (R&R). During this free period, I had a choice of going to Hawaii, or a number of Asian cities, including the Philippines or Singapore. Influenced by the feedback of some fellow marines who had made Singapore sound like an amazing place to go, I chose the Sensual House Hotel in Singapore.

Finally, after weeks of wearing my soiled jungle utilities, I cleaned up and got dressed in my civilian clothes. I then boarded a commercial plane in Da Nang, and arrived in Singapore on a Friday night. Since the lifespan for a Vietnam soldier was only thirty seconds, I opted to deplete my entire military savings account and filled my pockets. If this was my first and possibly last R&R, I wanted it to be one to remember. My pockets swelled even bigger after my American dollars were exchanged for 'sing,' short for Singapore's official currency, Singapore Dollar.

Singapore was absolutely beautiful and the hotel was picture perfect. A guy, perhaps the Maitre'd, had pre-arranged for five or six women to be at the hotel. Each woman was free of STDs, and had up-to-date shot cards as proof. In those times, prostituting women was common and acceptable for military men on R&R. That practice was nixed in 2006, when the U.S. Department of Defense established it a crime for a soldier to hire a prostitute. Penalties, if caught, include prison, forfeit of pay and dishonorable discharge.

Believe me when I tell you, making a selection between those beauties was difficult. While I was taking my time studying each one, I can't deny that my thoughts wandered to Sandra. However, she was more than 8,000 miles away and I was only nineteen, stressed and in need of some re-laxation. In addition, communications between us had consisted of only two letters. In one of my letters, I had taken time to describe my near death experiences in the war zone and how much I missed her, and of course, I asked about Francine. Her letter in return lacked any love or compassion, nothing like the true love letters that some of the other soldiers received. Parsons, from Virginia, had shown me pictures that his girlfriend had sent, but not one picture did I receive of Sandra nor my baby, Francine. I was out of sight and out of mind, or so I thought. I guess there is some truth to that old saying, "What the heart can't see, the heart can't love."

Parsons had spoken about me in his correspondence to his girlfriend and the next thing I knew, she'd written a letter addressed to me that included her picture. It was amazing the correspondence that I began to receive from the family members of my fellow marines. Still it was not the same as having letters from my own wife.

I received letters from my aunts, my sisters and some of their friends who also had their friends write me. The biggest news I received about Sandra was in a letter from my sister, Alice, who informed me that Sandra had left Mama's house and moved back home with her mother. I'm sure it was our baby Francine who promoted the reconciliation between Sandra and her Mom - just like grandbabies are known to do. I didn't harbor any ill feelings about Sandra moving, but I would have preferred that she had informed me instead of Alice.

It pleased me a great deal that the military was sending Sandra a portion of my earnings to help take care of Francine. Being that the average age of Vietnam soldiers was nineteen, most were single who had their entire paychecks to spend as they wished. However, as a married soldier, almost half of my pay was being sent home to my wife and child.

Returning my focus to the women before me, I realized that the other men in the lobby had been quick to choose. By now, all but one of the women were walking away, arm in arm, with their date. The maitre'd clapped his hands and suddenly, more women appeared. This time, I made a quick choice and Nisa from Malaysia became my companion for the week.

Pictured above, Herman with Nisa, his companion
during his R&R in Singapore.

I did not have a clear understanding about the value of
the U.S. Dollar and the conversion value of the Singapore
dollar. What I can say is that within a matter of three days,
I had managed to drain my pockets of all the money I had
brought with me. It was easy to get caught up in that exotic
haven where no weapons of any kind were allowed, thus, no
gunfire to be heard and no fear of attack by the enemy.

During my R & R, I made a connection with another soldier, Mitchell from Detroit. Together, he and his date and
Nisa and I had a blast. Although I was tempted to taste new
and foreign foods, I obeyed military orders to stick with

American dishes, foods that my stomach was familiar with, and of course, the *scrumptiously delicious* military's C-rations, which my system was reluctantly growing accustomed to.

Mitchell and I danced and dined with our compansions in the ballroom at the hotel. Outside of the hotel, we took the guided tour of Singapore and soaked up some sun at the beautiful white sand beaches. I had a great time in Singapore, and if only for one week, the horrors of the war zone had been pushed to the farthest part of my mind. The week went by fast; way too fast.

Pictured above, Herman (far right) with other soldiers while on R & R in Singapore.

▲ ▲ ▲

The memories of the fantastic week in Singapore faded too quickly as the routine of patrolling through desolate villages searching for the enemy, hijacked me back to my real purpose for being in Vietnam. One of the marines who traveled with our unit was an interpreter who spoke to the villagers, asking for information about the enemy's whereabouts. As a show of support, we offered our C-rations to let them know that the American soldiers were there to fight for them against the enemy who took their farm products and livestock.

The picture below shows me speaking with two North Vietnamese women with straw hats working in a rice paddy. Both women had black teeth due to the constant chewing of betel nut. It was said that the natural high from chewing betel nut provided energy for the long hours they spent working in the fields. Oddly, their toes were spread apart like hands, also due to the arduous work they had to perform while working in the rice paddies. In the picture below, I was offering them cigarettes, and chocolate from my C-rations, which they cheerfully accepted. I recall wondering if they could read English, would they still want the C-rations knowing that some of the cans were dated more than twenty years earlier, no doubt left over from World War II.

CHAPTER 16

▲ ▲ ▲

IN SPITE OF the shrapnel flying all around, I made it through the first ninety days of my tour without being hit. During the latter part of month three, September 25th to be exact, our unit was on patrol in the vicinity of Quang Tri, Republic of Vietnam (RVN). On this particular day, the enemy initiated a rocket attack. At the very moment a marine was yelling "incoming," the rockets were raining in. I scurried over to a nearby foxhole and dove in for cover. Within seconds, a burning sensation began searing through the upper extremity of my right arm. After closer observation, I realized I had just sustained my first wound - hot shrapnel from a rocket attack. The corpsman quickly applied pressure to stop the bleeding. Once he was sure the bleeding was under control, he bandaged me up. Amazingly, the burning sensation that I experienced upon impact diminished rather quickly. That was a true blessing, for it would be days later before I was taken by helicopter to the Naval Support Activity Station Hospital (NSA) on China Beach, in Da Nang, Vietnam. At the hospital, the shrapnel in my arm was removed. While I lay in bed for a brief recovery, I conversed with another soldier in the next bed. In the middle of the night, we spoke candidly about our wounds and I admitted, "I'm just glad it didn't hit me in my face or between my legs."

I occupied a hospital bed for only twenty-four hours, then was released. Upon my return to the field, I learned that I would receive a Purple Heart, a United States military decoration awarded in the name of the president to a soldier killed or wounded during battle.

The Purple Heart differs from all other decorations in that an individual is not recommended, but rather he or she is entitled for being wounded or killed while serving in any capacity with the U.S. Armed Services. Vice President Hubert H. Humphrey, who served from 1965 through 1969, had come to the hospital ship and presented various medals. I had just missed him. It would be months later during a presentation at Quantico when I received my Purple Heart.

CALL LETTERS: JBK *DSGR-41-S-838P PG DT* CHARGE TO: CAS GOVT

MRS. HERMAN L. WILLIAMS
214 LEVINE STREET,
WILLIAMSON, WEST VIRGINIA

THIS IS TO INFORM YOU THAT YOUR HUSBAND PRIVATE FIRST CLASS HERMAN L. WILLIAMS
USMC WAS INJURED ON 25 SEPTEMBER 1967 IN THE VICINITY OF QUANG TRI, REPUBLIC
OF VIETNAM. HE SUSTAINED A FRAGMENTATION WOUND TO THE RIGHT ARM FROM HOSTILE
ROCKET FIRE WHILE IN A DEFENSIVE POSITION. HE WAS TREATED IN THE FIELD AND
RETURNED TO DUTY. HIS CONDITION AND PROGNOSIS WERE EXCELLENT. IN VIEW OF THE
ABOVE NO FURTHER REPORTS WILL BE SENT TO YOU FROM THIS HEADQUARTERS. HIS
MAILING ADDRESS REMAINS THE SAME.

CHAPTER 17

— ▲ ▲ ▲ —

AROUND MID-OCTOBER, 1967, I was taken out of the field and sent to Da Nang for demolition training. This was not part of a rifleman's job, so I was surprised when I was the only one from our unit selected for this training. Over the next seven days, I was trained to blow up bunkers, booby traps, and demolition. The application used during training was underground tunnels which Vietnam was full of. Teakwood, being the strongest wood of any tree, was used to hold up the underground tunnels. I learned to wrap the explosives and set the detonator cord around the teakwood supports. Once the explosion goes off, it could cut right through a bunker and cave in the tunnel. Unless there was a rear exit, no one would be expected to survive.

The urgency of learning this training became clear sooner than I could have imagined. Upon my return to my unit, my platoon received orders to go on an operation in an area where intelligence had already reported that a number of booby traps had been detected. We started out avoiding the main (obvious) trail by creating our own trail. Our point man quickly discovered a trap and I was called over to dispose of it. It was a good thing that I could demonstrate my ability so soon while the training was still fresh in my mind. Being that this was my first time, I really wanted to produce a big bang!! Boom!!!

Using my razor sharp bayonet, I cleared the debris from the area around the booby trap. Carefully, I knelt down and went to work setting the demolition to explode. Minutes later, I yelled, "Fire in the hole." After setting the timer, I scurried over to join my crew. I had purposely overloaded the explosives just to make double damn sure when the explosion went off, there'd be no mistaking its damage. Not only did it blow up the booby trap that the enemy had originally intended for us, it also blew the cover off a 2,000 pound bomb that had been placed a few feet away. Calculating, they were indeed. However, those NVAs had underestimated the marines. This time, Lance Corporal Herman Williams had been ready for 'em!! After the explosion went off, I went back to check it out. I'd been taught, always go back and check.

"Williams, if you hadn't overloaded, that second bomb would have wiped us out! Excellent work!" said the platoon commander, slapping me on the back.

CHAPTER 18

▲ ▲ ▲

On December 16, 1967, I was promoted to a Corporal-E4, a noncommissioned officer. A commissioned officer must attend officers candidate school (OCS) at Quantico and be trained for a leadership/officer position. Becoming a non-commissioned officer meant that I had moved through the ranks and my performance met the criteria, particularly, my leadership and training of new recruits.

▲ ▲ ▲

Vietnam is eleven hours ahead of Washington, D.C. Like the United States, the Vietnamese celebrate Christmas on December 25, and New Year's Day on January 1. The exception is during a Lunar New Year, in which case the celebration begins later in January.

The Tet Offensive of 1968, one of the largest military campaigns of the Vietnam War, was named The Tet Offensive after the Vietnamese Lunar New Year, when the fighting began on January 30, 1968. Based on historical accounts of this war, more than 70,000 North Vietnam and Viet Cong forces initiated a series of attacks on more than

100 cities and towns in South Vietnam, including the city of Hue.

Unit 2/4 was set up near Dong Ha, north of Hue, when we received the order to saddle up because the NVA had overrun Hue. We jumped on the sixbye military trucks and started down Highway 1. When we arrived, I remember us staring at the sky in amazement. Even though it was night time, the sky above was a blazing bright yellow. For a brief moment, I recalled the city's beauty. The Catholic schools and churches that I had previously admired, were now in ruins. The utter destruction before my eyes was unbelievable. And, considering that the NVA had bombed this city on the most sacred holiday was sacrilegious. In addition, the NVA had crossed the boundaries, as the city of Hue was not even a jungle warfare area.

Unit 2/4 immediately went to work as the blocking force to prevent further destruction by the NVA. We went house to house, and building to building. Although we'd been trained for all types of combat in buildings, up until this point, our experience had only been in the bush.

Fighting in other areas during the Tet Offensive lasted about a week or less. However, the Battle of Hue lasted close to thirty days. It was reported that more than 5,000 civilians were killed in this battle. Approximately 150 U.S. marines and 400 South Vietnamese troops also lost their lives. An additional 3,000 were reported missing.

On the communist side, more than 5,000 soldiers were killed by U.S. and ARVN forces during this battle.

The Tet Offensive of 1968, was a turning point after which President Lyndon B. Johnson initiated talks to end U.S. troops fighting in the Vietnam War. Negotiations would play out another five years. It was Johnson's successor, President Richard Nixon, who brought U.S. troops home from the Vietnam War, just prior to his resignation in 1974. Finally in 1975, President Gerald Ford declared an end to the war in Vietnam. In spite of the high number of casualties, somehow I made it through.

CHAPTER 19

△ △ △

TWICE DURING OUR numerous operations, Unit 2/4 lost so many men that it became necessary to regroup. On one occasion, our entire unit boarded the USS Iwo Jima, a converted aircraft carrier, and headed across the South China Sea towards the Philippines. Upon arrival, our goal was to secure additional reinforcements.

Just to see the shoreline, after all the destruction we'd seen back in the war zone of Vietnam, was an awesome sight to behold! When we docked at the pier of the Subic Bay Naval Base, we immediately made our way to meet recruits from the Special Landing Force (SLF). To explain it simply, the SLF was like a training facility that provided additional troops to units like 2/4. The assignment at hand was for Unit 2/4 to provide *additional* jungle training, before taking these recruits back to the actual killing fields of Vietnam. Over the next five days, these recruits, average age of nineteen, received the most comprehensive and intense jungle training that we could possibly offer. This training assignment was crucial due to the high number of casualties.

During this brief stint to the Philippines, I had the unexpected pleasure of reconnecting with an old friend. Ronald Blackwell and I hadn't seen each other since boot camp, so imagine my surprise when I saw him at the chow hall. Turns out, after his leg injury which he sustained during boot camp, Ronald became a chef with the Marine Corps and was now stationed in the Philippines.

Upon leaving the main gate of the Subic Bay Naval Base, I had to cross over the "Shit River" bridge. This river was so named because of its awful smell. I actually had to hold my breath each time I crossed over the bridge. And if the smell wasn't bad enough, the situation was exacerbated when I witnessed children actually swimming in that shit hole and begging for coins from the servicemen who crossed over.

Across the bridge was the heart of Olangapo City and the "night" life every serviceman was drawn to experience, at least once. Olangapo City had night clubs and skivvy houses galore and its main source of income was from the American servicemen who patronized the area.

That evening, I met Ronald in Olangapo City in an area called "the jungle." This area was mostly frequented by the black soldiers. Over a couple of beers, we sat and reminisced about Williamson and what we'd both been up to since boot camp. He also introduced me to his girlfriend, a native of the Philippines whose name escapes me now.

On the same evening that I reconnected with Ronald from my past, I also had the pleasure of making an acquaintance with someone new *and* beautiful. I was on shore patrol duty and armed with my 45. As a corporal, I was responsible for looking out for the servicemen to make sure they didn't go to any of the off-limits joints, like the more dangerous skivvy houses.

The Soul Club was filled to capacity, mostly with servicemen either dancing, drinking or smiling into the face of a pretty girl. Through the crowd, I caught a glimpse of the most beautiful girl that I'd seen since arriving in the Philippines. Instantly, I knew I had to meet her. As I made my way through the crowd towards her table, the other guy she was with came into view. Being confident in my uniform, corporal stripes projecting, I continued until I reached their table and made my bold approach. "What you doing with that old dude?"

I was not prepared for her reproach. "You should not be disrespectful." Her expression was disapproving, and admittedly, she was right. I'd been bold when I took my chance at getting her attention, but my attempt had been taken as disrespectful. Feeling only *slightly* rejected, I turned away and walked to the juke box. After scanning the various American artists, I deposited my quarter and selected, "I Can't Stay Away From You." As The Impressions and Curtis Mayfield began to croon, and I began to sway with the rhythm, I turned my gaze towards her and smiled. What happened next was nothing short of magical. It had to be, for I was surprised to see her making her way through the crowd. The girl got prettier with each step that she took towards me. This time there was no scolding in her voice. "You play that? You play that? That's my song. How did you know that?"

"How could I know? It must be fate," I suggested with a grin. Whether it was fate, an amazing coincidence, or simply the *con* that many of the girls played on the servicemen, I wasn't sure. My uncertainty gained clarity over the next five days as Brenda and I spent every available moment together. I even invited her to the base and introduced her to my fellow marines. Brenda was so pretty, that one of my superiors offered me $100 just to take a picture with her. When I relayed his offer to Brenda, and she rejected it, my heart swelled with pride. It was also confirmation that she had found a place in her heart for me, as she had found a place in mine.

Although my first encounter with Brenda was brief, it was all so special. We both felt it. On three more occasions, I had the opportunity to return to the Philippines. Each time it was Brenda and me, together.

When I returned to the world, stateside, I was surprised and pleased when I was told by another soldier that he'd seen my picture with Brenda hanging on the wall at the Soul Club. Incidentally, the Soul Club just happened to be owned by Brenda's mother.

CHAPTER 20

▲ ▲ ▲

I WAS WELL into the second half of my tour in Vietnam with countless missions and operations behind me. Dead soldiers and flying shrapnel were constant. Although I had sustained one wound, I intended to complete my tour with no fear of the future to come. I can honestly say, my "will" to be the best that I could be, kept me in the most positive frame of mind. With every new mission, my confidence maintained and I never doubted myself or my superiors. I never questioned their orders because I knew with all my training, I could carry out any order they gave me. I was pumped.

▲ ▲ ▲

Around the latter part of March, 1968, our unit had set up around the (DMZ). Funny thing was, we could look through our binoculars and see the enemy as they stared right back through their binoculars. Although the DMZ was declared a neutral zone, it didn't stop the enemy from firing at us.

Around the latter part of April, 1968, I received orders to go out on a two man listening post with Private Johnson. We set up 200 meters in front of our line to listen with an electronic probe that I stuck in the ground. The device was similar to a set of headphones and was so sensitive, it had the ability to detect sounds of activity moving about. Any movement, like large weaponry or a large unit approaching, could definitely be detected.

Private Johnson was the look-out man, while I listened intently with the probe. Every thirty minutes, base command would check in on us by radio which was turned down very low. "Hotel 1 Alpha, if all is secure, key your hand set once." Every half hour, the number of keys would be changed to confuse the enemy, who were undoubtedly listening.

Clearly, what I heard that night were the vibrations of a huge activity. Back in the rear, I reported our findings. I would later suspect that it was the enemy setting up in the Village of Dai Do.

The following day, I was told to take a squad associated with Hotel Company to the village of Dong Huen, for what was supposed to be a routine patrol. There should have been twelve soldiers in my squad, but we were short five men. To keep it as simple as possible, the Battle of Dai Do, also known as the Battle of Dong Ha, took place along 1.5 miles of territory along the Cua Viet River. This territory consisted of five hamlets: Dong Huen, An Lac, Thung Do, Dinh To, and the largest hamlet, Dai Do. These hamlets were situated approximately 500 meters between each other.

Obeying my orders, I lead my squad of seven marines towards Dong Huen. I would later learn that four different companies had been dispatched from all sides of the village. Our unit, Hotel Company, was dispatched from the west. Before we reached the village, we came upon an open clearing, an apparent graveyard, with numerous pyramid type mounds. Contrary to burials in the United States, the dead in Vietnam are buried standing up.

Our point man who was approximately twenty yards in front, suddenly beckoned me to come forward. "Corporal Williams, I see the enemy!"

I moved up to take a look for myself. Once I reached the point man, I confirmed that the enemy, North Vietnamese forces, was moving about. At this time, I decided to flank the enemy and dispatched three men to the right flank of the village. As they disappeared from sight, weapons suddenly fired and it was on. I yelled out to my men, "Is everything alright?"

"I am okay, brother. I am okay."

At that point, I didn't know if my men had been killed or not. What I knew for sure was that the broken English reply was conveyed by none other than the enemy. Pissed off by this obvious ploy, I lashed out, "Later for you, Charlie!"

A brief exchange of fire erupted between both sides. Other companies were moving through each of the smaller hamlets dodging heavy fire as they moved towards the largest of the hamlets, Dai Do.

Within minutes, Hotel 1 Alpha was in serious trouble. NVA were firing their AK47s from the hip. They were popping up from their spider holes on the outside of their hooches where they could drop back down out of sight, lickety split. I threw a grenade and immediately, it came right back and exploded just yards away from me. Radio man was with me. "Stay down!" I warned. More grenades hurled through the air from both sides leaving wounded marines and NVA all over the ground.

Within seconds of the grenade exploding, five of the seven soldiers were wounded and crawling on their stomachs towards me. "Just stay down and keep crawling," I ordered and pointed to the left, beckoning them in the direction I assumed our help would come. I had already radioed for help. "Hotel 1, we are taking on heavy fire. Request support, request support!" In response, two other companies consolidated their position to assist.

Fire continued hitting all around us and another explosion blasted. Seconds later, through the haze, more dead bodies were scattered all over the ground. Some of the bodies were the enemy and some were marines. Adrenaline was surging through my body, and I just knew in another thirty seconds they'd have me too.

▲ ▲ ▲

My second wound felt like I'd been hit with someone's fist. Radio Man spoke just above a whisper. "Corporal Williams, you've been hit. You're bleeding!" I turned in time to see an

NVA hightailing away with weapon in hand. I knew it was his weapon that had wounded me.

As I was being carried away, I passed a number of dead marines. Amongst the dead was Lieutenant Shortenton. He'd been hit by a grenade and now lay dead with half of his jaw blown off. Lieutenant Shortenton was from New York. We'd held conversations about this and that and had gotten tight enough that I could tease him. Especially when he returned from a week of R & R and informed me that he'd married his girlfriend. "What you go and do that for?" I had teased. Truthfully, I was really happy for him.

I was medevaced to the USS Princeton, an aircraft carrier now serving as a military hospital during the Vietnam War. Of all places, I had sustained a gunshot wound to my left buttock.

Upon arrival to the Princeton, I was given a shot of morphine, and the medical staff proceeded to cut off my jungle pants. As I lay on my stomach, they sprayed my wound with a water hose, after which the doctor proceeded to stitch me with wire. Amazingly, I didn't feel any pain. I just laid there with my head buried in my arms, thankful that my wound was minor, at least compared to some of my fellow marines. I'd been only a few feet away from Lieutenant Shortenton, and it could have easily been me lying there, dead. Again, my Creator had saved me. I'm not sure how many of the seven men in my squad survived, but all of us, for sure, had been wounded.

Since joining the Marines, I've had the awesome opportunity to meet people from numerous nationalities, including a true American Indian. Unfortunately, my first sight of an Indian was while he lay unconscious with numerous wounds over his body which I perceived to be from an explosion, a grenade or mortar. The Indian was not a member of my platoon, but he was a marine attached to Unit 2/4.

▲ ▲ ▲

That night, after the doctor had triaged us, a solemn male voice came through the intercom. Most likely, the voice belonged to the chaplain. "God bless the marines on shore. God bless the marines who are in our care. God bless the souls of the marines who have died in battle." The voice continued, calling out the names of the dead. The list was long and included my lieutenant, John Shortenton. Upon hearing the lieutenant's name, I suddenly felt a tremendous sense of loss, greater than any other death that I'd encountered since my tour of duty began in Vietnam.

▲ ▲ ▲

Three days later, with wire stitches in my left buttock, I was released from the USS Princeton. Surprisingly, the stitches didn't hamper my movement. The American soldiers were still heavily engaged in combat, trying to gain control of the NVA soldiers. Sadly, the number of able-bodied American soldiers was rapidly decreasing in numbers, either killed in action or wounded.

With Lieutenant Shortenton now dead, I was the most senior marine in my squad at that time. Having more combat experience than the others, I felt that I couldn't let them down. They had already shown me that they trusted me, and being a marine with a purpose, I intended to return to the battle with a real burning desire to kick some ass. Reflecting back, my only explanation was the adrenaline, that amazing hormone that triggers the body to fight or flight in stressful situations. For sure, my adrenaline had been working overtime, for I was ready to fight, ready to kick some ass. So ready, I couldn't even recognize that I was returning to the battle with my own ass in stiches. How crazy was that!

Herman pictured above with bandage covering his wound.

It wasn't until much later, after returning to the states, that I learned a soldier is usually sent away from the war zone after sustaining two wounds. I can only speculate that the shortage of men is the reason I remained in Vietnam, after sustaining my second wound.

Near the end of the Battle of Dai Do, around May 5, 1968, the Magnificent Bastards were credited with killing hundreds of NVA. Of its own soldiers, approximately 525 were wounded or killed. More importantly, the Marines were victorious in preventing the NVA from attacking the Dong Ha combat base.

I have read several published articles and a book, *The Magnificent Bastards*, by Keith Nolan, pertaining to the Battle of Dai Do. As one who participated and survived that brutal battle, I've read page after page with fascination and familiarity, reliving critical moments as my own actions were noted, even though, my name was never mentioned.

Regardless of whether my name was mentioned or not, I have a feeling that the authors of the numerous publications surrounding the horrendous Battle of Dai Do can validate that I am blessed to be a survivor with the opportunity to share this amazing testimony. I owe it all to my Creator.

▲ ▲ ▲

Recently, during the 239th birthday celebration of the Marine Corps held on 11-3-2014, in Philadelphia, the Magnificent

Bastards were mentioned as a unit most deserving to be recognized by a Presidential Unit Citation (PUC) for its contributions to the victory of the Battle of Dai Do.

▲ ▲ ▲

After my release from the hospital, I took the opportunity to stroll around China Beach. I was approached by some beautiful girls who tempted me to patronize them at a skivvy house. This for sure was a rare opportunity that I didn't want to miss. However, upon entering the doorway of the skivvy house, who did I run into but my 6 foot 5, half-brother, Darrel. It had been three years since we had seen each other last. "What you doing here, man?" I asked in surprise.

"What am I doing in Vietnam, or what am I doing here?" Darryl replied and we both bowled over in laughter. Needless to say, the need to reminisce became more important than the girls, so we left the house in search of a beer. Although I had no idea that Darrel was in Vietnam, he had already heard I'd been wounded and was angry on account of it. After a long discussion, we hugged and promised each other that we'd remain safe, so we could see each other again back in the world. Fortunately, Darrel made it through the Vietnam War without suffering any physical wounds

▲ ▲ ▲

Back in the states, for the second time, Mama had answered the door to the military officials who once again gave her the news that I had been wounded, but fortunately had survived.

▲ ▲ ▲

The stitches in my buttocks were removed sometime later by a corpsman during our down time at one of the base camps.

CHAPTER 21

▲ ▲ ▲

"LEAVE ME, LEAVE me," the wounded marine cried out in agony. It was Parsons and he'd been hit. I locked eyes with my friend, Lobo, a rifleman on my fire team from Oakland, California. Lobo was about 6 foot 2, and weighed 225 pounds. We were just inches away from Parsons and upon closer observance, we noticed he'd been hit in at least three places. Together, Lobo and I dragged him to the medevac that was waiting not far away.

I climbed aboard the chopper and accompanied Parsons to the hospital in Da Nang. "Hang in there, man. Hang in there," I pleaded. Parsons was a short timer, almost finished his entire tour. To end up killed in action (KIA) this late in the war would have been the ultimate tragedy. Rarely did we learn the status of the wounded. They'd be taken out of the bush and we'd never hear from them again. Thus was the case with Parsons. I never learned whether or not he survived.

▲ ▲ ▲

I returned to my unit aboard a skimmer boat, speeding along the Cua Viet River. There was food, meat and bread, aboard which I stuffed into all the pockets of my jungle utilities to take back to my men. I knew they'd love a break from the ham and lima beans in our C-rations which they had renamed "ham and motherfuckers." Mainly because no one liked them. Sometimes, we'd throw in some cheese to make them bearable. Of all the foods in our C-rations, the spaghetti and meatballs was the most passable. The pound cake was pretty good. Sometimes I'd spread peanut butter over mine, thus renaming it "peanut butter cake."

▲ ▲ ▲

Back in the bush, I reconnected with Lobo and found that he'd taken a hit in the knee. It didn't stop him from continuing, but once he was treated at the hospital, I didn't see him again until I left Vietnam and went to Oakland, California. There I reconnected with Lobo and he introduced me to his family. I was so happy he'd made it out alive.

▲ ▲ ▲

During another operation, the orders for the day sent our unit on a blocking force mission for a company of marines who were coming in on an Amtrak tank (an amphibious troop carrier.) As the marines from another unit were forcing the enemy in our direction, Unit 2/4 was to wipe them out as they pushed towards us. Unfortunately, the enemy had inflicted so many casualties who were approaching from the sea that our initial mission to block force turned into an all out search and destroy mission. Anything walking or running was the order.

Even though there was firing all around and shrapnel hitting my helmet, what really remained in my mind was not all the dead marine casualties and dead villagers. By now, those images had become an everyday occurrence. What was unusual about that day was an old woman who had caught my attention. The search and destroy order had come a little late, and I made the decision not to kill her. There was devastation all around and she was just standing amongst a lot of dead bodies, helpless and harmless. Her shoulders were drooping and I could see the sadness in her eyes.

After we pulled back out of the village, I could hear the jets flying above, on the way back in for a final bombing run. The compassion that I felt for the old woman caught me by surprise. Perhaps she reminded me of my own grandmother, I don't know. I didn't have time to dwell on it.

Although I had obliged the silent plea in the old woman's eyes, the pilots spared her not. As they flew over the village releasing napalm canisters, all remaining living creatures were killed, including the old woman.

CHAPTER 22

$$\blacktriangle \blacktriangle \blacktriangle$$

ON MAY 2, 1968, I was considered a short timer with only two more months to fulfill my thirteen month tour of duty. I had no idea how many missions and operations I'd fought in, but I was aware that the number of casualties was extremely high. Although wounded twice myself, I was still alive and engaged.

It was hot and muggy. I had endured the extreme heat and the monsoon season when it had rained more days than I could recall. Easter had come and gone. I don't know who to thank. Perhaps it was the mother of one of the soldiers or one of the many extraordinary people who cared and took the time to send us care baskets. Whoever it was sent a basket filled with Easter eggs - colored eggs at that.

We had no sooner finished the blocking force operation along the Cua Viet River when we were assigned a big regimental size operation to sweep the enemy, again near the Cua Viet River. Army helicopters were flying overhead to cover us. I could see the enemy, an NVA shooting from a big machine gun. I believe I must have put about twenty rounds in him before I realized I'd already killed him. There was no more fire coming from his machine gun. He was simply frozen in position, like a statue.

A few feet away, a shrill went through the air that sent my blood cold. It was Thompson, crying out, "Mamaaaaaa." By the time his scream faded to a mere whisper, he was dead. Since our backpacks were loaded with ammunition and supplies, I remember crawling out of a hole with intentions of confiscating Thompson's food, water, weapon and ammo. His face was changing colors, fast. All of a sudden, I felt something hot hit me above my left eye. Boy had I made a grave mistake, giving up my position. The consequences was soon revealed as I covered my eye trying to hold back the hot blood that was rapidly seeping over my left eye.

The only form of transportation from our mission point to the hospital was aboard skimmer boats. Twenty minutes later, the boat hit shore where doctors were already waiting to treat the wounded. Of all the doctors who could have been on shore, this one just happened to recognize me from before. "Williams, this will be your third heart. You're going back 'to the world.' Get him out of here!"

I probably should have been relieved, but I was still in combat mode, filled with adrenaline.

I was medevaced to the USS Princeton. Following a brief stay, I was immediately sent to the marine base in Okinawa, Japan. Just like that, my tour of duty in Vietnam was over. Less than sixty days short of my full thirteen month tour.

From Okinawa, I was supposed to return to the states reverse style, but I was delayed by one day. After being in the bush for so long, it was important that I be free of any disease. Therefore, it was necessary that I undergo a series of blood tests. The initial results showed that my blood was elevated. Consequently, more blood work was ordered causing me to stay overnight. One of the nurse aides who held my hand commented, "Your hands, same same bamboo." Little did I know, this condition that affected both my hands and feet, would affect me for years to come.

On the following day, June 12, 1968, my tests results came back negative, and I was free to go. Shortly thereafter, I hopped aboard a Gov Air plane at the Kadena Air Force Base in Okinawa, heading back to the states.

CHAPTER 23

───── ▲ ▲ ▲ ─────

"LADIES AND GENTLEMEN, we have just been cleared to land at LAX, Los Angeles International Airport," announced the pilot, awaking me from my snooze. I strained my neck to peer out of the plane's tiny window for a glance at the parade of people that I *thought* would be waiting to welcome us back stateside. The plane made a smooth touch down on the runway and began to taxi towards the gate. Seconds later, with the gate in view, the pilot abruptly turned the plane. Minutes later we were ascending back into the air.

Chatter suddenly filled the cabin as the passengers uttered their confusion. Although we were baffled, to say the least, the pilot quickly put us as ease. We were being rerouted to the Marine Corps Air Station (MCAS) in El Toro, California. This sudden change was to avoid anti-Vietnam demonstrations that were underway at the airport.

▲ ▲ ▲

Later on the nightly news, I struggled to digest the perspective of the protestors. "End The War in Vietnam Now!" and "Make Love Not War," were amongst the hundreds of signs that they held up for the TV viewers to see. The reference to Vietnam soldiers being "baby killers" hit especially hard, flaring my emotions. Suddenly, the honor of my three Purple Hearts bounced in my mind from pride to shame and back. For the blood that I spilled on a foreign land for my country, this is what I returned to? What a rude awakening. I would later discover that this "unwelcome" experience triggered my silent wound, Post Traumatic Stress Disorder (PTSD.)

▲ ▲ ▲

With my tour of duty in Vietnam behind me, my new duty station, Marine Corps Base Quantico, was located near Triangle, Virginia, approximately fifty miles from Washington, D.C. Quantico is the marine base where the U.S. President's helicopter, Marine 1, is stored. It also serves as the location for Marine Corps officer candidate training.

Prior to reporting for work duty, I was permitted a thirty day leave. During this period of freedom, I decided to visit some of my relatives, starting with Aunt Joyce, who lived relatively close in the D.C. area. Aunt Joyce had been so proud of me, and had sent word for me to come and visit.

During my short visit with Aunt Joyce, I connected with some fellow marines to celebrate our return, "back to the world." We saluted each other over libations, mainly Thunderbird, that we purchased from the Central Liquor Store at 9th and F Streets. Fortunately, I'd had the good sense to take a taxi back to Aunt Joyce's. Unfortunately, my haste from her front door to her bathroom proved to be futile, for what spilled from my cupped hands overflowed in a disastrous trail onto Aunt Joyce's white carpet. If there was any way that I could redeem myself, I knew it wouldn't be that day. The disappointed look in her eyes spelled it out, loud and clear. In no uncertain terms, I had overstayed my welcome. I didn't wait around for her to ask me to leave.

▲ ▲ ▲

During my tour of duty in Vietnam, Mama had received a total of three visits from military officials who came to deliver news about my wounds. Even though I knew she was proud of me for my service as a marine, I also knew my wounds had caused her daily stress and worry. To make it up to her, I wanted to surprise her by showing up dressed in full uniform and draped with all my ribbons. I wanted her to see me in the flesh, whole and well, with her own two eyes.

It was June, 1968, when I arrived in Williamson. I returned by Greyhound, the same way I left. Indeed I had missed my hometown and decided to take in the sights on foot, instead of hailing a taxi. As I walked and inhaled the fresh air, it struck me that I'd been across the world and returned full circle - grateful that I had made it back alive - sad that so many of my fellow marines had not.

Walking slowly down Third Avenue, word was spreading fast, "Jerry is home." Merchants from various businesses appeared at their doorway to salute me and welcome me back. Some took time to holla, "Jerry, you sure look good in your uniform." I smiled and waved, but I didn't linger. They knew I was trying to get home to Mama.

At the end of Third Avenue, I turned left onto Vincent Street, heading towards the viaduct. As I walked underneath, my nostrils were engulfed with the pungent odor of the damp musty cement. On the other side of the viaduct, the houses came into view. I thought it odd that they seemed smaller than I remembered. Suddenly, I was flooded with memories from my childhood and hanging out with my friends at some of these houses.

Pictured above is the home in Williamson, West Virginia, where Herman was raised.

As I continued down Vincent Street, my heart rate quickened. With only one more block to go, I began to wonder if Mama would even be home, so I could carry out my intent to surprise her. Finally, reaching the corner of LeVine Street, I saw her sitting on her front porch. She had on a white sweater and was rocking back and forth in the old white rocker. My heart suddenly ached for Daddy and I wished he were sitting there beside her, so I could surprise both of them.

About fifty yards from her sidewalk entrance, Mama looked up and her eyes focused on me walking towards her. She stood up slowly and walked to the edge of the porch. With tears welling up in her eyes, she sang, "*There he is, there he is.*"

I wrapped my arms around Mama and lifted her off her feet. When I finally let her down, she rushed inside and returned with her favorite glass pitcher, the one she brought out of the cupboard for special occasions.

"Where is Alice?" I asked after gulping down a tall glass of Mama's ice cold lemonade.

Mama smiled through her tears. "I am so proud to say that your sister, Alice, is graduating today from Williamson High School."

"Williamson High?" I asked, perplexed. "Not Liberty?"

"Nope. Not Liberty. There is *no* more Liberty High School," Mama said shaking her head, sadness in her eyes. I could barely comprehend what Mama was saying, although she was very clear about it. *The school that I had loved, had been closed?*

"No. Couldn't be." I uttered. "That makes no sense. So many nights I've dreamed of returning to Liberty and sharing my experiences with Mrs. Glover and the other teachers and Coach Starling..." I trailed off, unable to explain the true core of my feelings to Mama. Returning to Liberty was extremely important for my psychological being. I needed to return to the place and time before the horrors of the Vietnam War exploded from Pandora's Box. I needed to once again see the school where I had spent the last six years of my school days, from 7th through 12th grades. Like the other soldiers who had come to Liberty and made presentations, I was preparing to do the same thing. I needed to see the teachers and Coach Starling. I wanted to feel their hugs and see the pride in their eyes that I had become a marine and survived three wounds with honor. At the very core of my being, I needed to feel that sense of security and innocence of my childhood days. I was surprised by the sudden ache that engulfed me as I realized I'd never fulfill all those yearnings. Those dreams had suddenly shattered into a million pieces. To me, it felt as though my whole squad had gone and left me to fight all alone.

Although I should have headed over to Williamson High for Alice's graduation with Mama, I was traumatized with the news about Liberty. Perhaps my reaction had to do with the PTSD kicking in. In any case, to return to Williamson and find there was no Liberty was devastating.

Later that evening, Alice and I sat on the porch reminiscing. I tried to keep my feelings about Liberty's closing to a minimum. After all, today was a happy day for her. I remembered the happiness that I felt on my graduation day and didn't want to spoil hers. Alice did offer the only explanation she knew about the school closing. "The powers that be made a decision to close Liberty, part of the Civil Rights desegregation movement."

▲ ▲ ▲

On the following day, I reconnected with some of the fellas who provided more updates on who was still in Williamson and who had left. My friend, Terry Warren, had returned to Williamson from Connecticut and was the proud owner of a '64 Chevy. Although I hadn't yet obtained my driver's license, he handed me the keys just because I asked. How that turned out for him was an irresponsible error in judgement. He soon realized that after I ran smack into a pole leaving a huge dent on the left side of his Chevy's fender. My attitude about the dent was, "Aw man, don't worry about it. I got you covered." Fortunately, Terry was forgiving and later that day, he drove me to see my baby girl and my wife who were still staying in Matewan with Sandra's mother.

Although Sandra and I were legally married, and I looked respectable showing up in my Marine Corps uniform, my mother-in-law was having no part of me staying overnight under her roof. This cold-water-in-my-face message, was delivered by Sandra who had returned from her mother's bedroom where she remained out of sight during my brief visit. I thought it odd, very odd, that I had never met my mother-in-law face to face. Not even on our wedding day. Surely, she wasn't still upset with me for getting her daughter pregnant, I pondered. We had done the right thing by getting married, and certainly I was no dead beat dad, as the military was sending my wife and baby a big portion of my check every month. I was just twenty years old and had survived three wounds during the Vietnam War. However, unlike most people who thanked me for serving our country, my mother-in-law did not come out of her room to greet me at all. With no place of my own, my idea for a family reunion would be briefer than planned. Thanks to Terry, who still had my back, Sandra and I piled into his car with our baby girl. He drove us to the nearest hotel which, at that time, was in Huntington, West Virginia, close to fifty miles away.

After checking in at the hotel, I held and kissed on my sweet baby girl, Francine. She was now fifteen months old. She seemed happy and well taken care of. When she smiled at me, I was elated with the knowledge that she was my baby and I was the father who had brought her into this world.

Time and distance had certainly made for an awkward reunion for Sandra and me. Still, I was glad to see her and spend what little time we could together with our daughter.

Two days later we headed to the Greyhound bus station. We kissed, said our goodbyes and went our separate ways. I boarded a bus heading to Quantico to begin my new duties, and Sandra and Francine boarded another bus returning to their home in Matewan.

It would be many years later, on another trip to Williamson, before I would finally meet my mother-in-law Helen, face-to-face, for the very first time. I was visiting Francine who was an adult at the time and a mother of her own two girls, my granddaughters.

Pictured from left to right: Granddaughter Alexis; daughter Francine; Francine's husband, Marvin; granddaughter Mary and Herman

Francine had a new home built right down the street from her grandmother, Helen. When Francine asked me to join her and her uncle to make a quick visit to her grandmother's, I decided to go. *What the heck*, I thought. I might get lucky this time.

My decision to go proved to be a good one. Standing in the doorway, Francine did the honors. "Grandma, I'd like you to meet my father." Helen extended her hand towards my outstretched one, and we shook.

"I hope you plan to share some dinner with us," she said politely.

"I can eat," I admitted.

After our meal, Helen admitted to me that she had misjudged me and didn't know that I was the person that I was. To assure her that I had no misgivings, I later made her a mother of pearl statue of Jesus. I was pleased to learn that the statue remained on display in her living room until she passed away several years later.

CHAPTER 24

$\blacktriangle\blacktriangle\blacktriangle$

UPON MY ARRIVAL at Quantico, I was ranked a corporal, non-commission, educational NCO. Although I had heard about the civil unrest in Washington, D.C., due partly to the assassination of Martin Luther King, Jr., it was sad to think that I had returned from a war all the way overseas in Vietnam and returned to the states, to find our nation's capital in distress. I sat in the passenger seat of the jeep alongside a sergeant. We rode through D.C. observing the burnt out liquor stores and other businesses that had been looted. In an effort to control further looting and destruction of property, a strict curfew had been imposed throughout the city. As we continued our drive, I absorbed harassing insults from young black rioters who focused their anger at me as though I was the one responsible for killing MLK. From the Vietnam War to guarding the nation's capital. Seriously? It was a hard scenario to comprehend.

$\blacktriangle\blacktriangle\blacktriangle$

At Quantico, I also served as an educational NCO, managing college and training records for marines.

Shortly after reporting to Quantico, I received a memo requesting my attendance at a formal presentation. On the designated day, I joined a number of other marines to receive our various awards. "Recipient of three Purple Hearts, Corporal Herman L. Williams," announced the speaker. I heard someone behind me gasp in amazement, "He got three Purple Hearts?" I don't recall any other marine receiving three Purple Hearts that day, so my recognition was extra special.

▲ ▲ ▲

Since returning from the Vietnam War and my near death experiences, strengthening my relations with my family had become very important to me. My duty at Quantico was like a normal eight hour day, from 08:00 to 16:30, Monday through Friday. This left my weekends free to travel and visit relatives and friends. Always on the go, like my tour in Vietnam. Always on the go.

During that first year at Quantico, I made several weekend trips to Warren, Ohio, where I developed a closer relationship with my biological mother, Cora Mae; her husband, Amos; and my sister, Margaret. While Alice and I had been raised by our grandparents, Margaret grew up with our mother and her father in Warren, Ohio.

It was my stepfather, Amos, who brought an end to my many trips, to and from on the Greyhound bus. Having served in the Army himself, Amos was very proud of me and gifted me generously with my very first vehicle, a '63

Chevrolet. The car was in good condition – shiny black with a 409 engine and convertible top. Oh, how I loved that car. Once I drove my Chevy to Connecticut, and some Puerto Ricans shouted out "hippity hop" because the hydraulics in the springs made the car bounce. I responded with a thumbs up.

▲ ▲ ▲

My biological father, James Small, married a lady named Ruby. Through their union, eight children were born. During my younger years in Williamson, they'd come to visit with relatives. It was during those summer visits that I bonded with my siblings, seven brothers and one sister.

Over the years, several of my brothers have passed away. Two are still living, Harold in Zanesville, Ohio, and Tony in Columbus, Ohio. My sister, Jamie, also resides in Columbus, Ohio.

I also made a visit to see my Aunt Geneva and Uncle Alfred at their twenty acre farm in North Carolina. Aunt Geneva's daughter, Sharon, and I share the same birthday, July 20, and fondly greet each other, "Hey 720." During our youth, we saw each other during summer months and holidays and our bond is still strong today.

Then there was my Aunt Phyllis and Uncle Jeff who lived in D.C. Uncle Jeff owned his own taxi cab which he drove on occasion back to Williamson, during the holidays. Although Aunt Phyllis and Uncle Jeff have passed away, I still honor them in my memories. My relationship with their daughter, Sylvia, and her daughter, Tracy, is still very strong.

▲ ▲ ▲

After Alice graduated from high school, she and Mama made a life changing decision to leave Williamson, West Virginia. Together they moved to Bridgeport, Connecticut, to be near other relatives.

▲ ▲ ▲

During the spring of 1970, I received a call from Sandra who informed me that she was planning to file for a divorce. I guess I'd have to say that distance and immaturity brought us to this point. There was no reason to contest it, so I didn't and the divorce became final.

CHAPTER 25

AFTER ABOUT A year at Quantico, I requested a transfer to Camp Pendleton, California. In my new position, I served as a transitional officer in casual company. Primarily, my duties consisted of escorting marines who were transitioning out of the military. I also escorted unruly marines to the brig who chose not to confirm. After time served, I'd escort them to the exit gate. I served in this role until I was discharged.

Initially, I voluntarily enlisted into the Marine Corps for four years. As a result of the three wounds I sustained in Vietnam, I was eligible for an early out. After giving it some thought, I decided to accept the early out and my honorable discharge after three years and thirty-seven days.

On September 29, 1972, I received my official honorable discharge from the U.S. Marine Corps, and the following awards were added to my military records:

- Combat Action Ribbon
- Marine Corps Good Conduct Medal
- National Defense Service Medal
- Navy Unit Commendation Ribbon with 1 Bronze star

- (3) Purple Heart Medals with 2 Gold stars
- Vietnam Service Medal – with 4 Bronze stars
- Marine Corps Sharpshooter Rifle Badge
- Republic of Vietnam Campaign Medal
- Republic of Vietnam MUC Gallantry Cross Foreign

Psychologically, I felt ready to detach myself from the military and pursue a regular job like a regular everyday citizen. I had taken a lot of abuse from the public and even from some of the marines who had not experienced the "pleasure" of serving in Vietnam. Had I known, I would end up with PTSD, perhaps I would have stayed and made a career in the military. At least, I would have been amongst men of my own kind.

CHAPTER 26

$\blacktriangle\,\blacktriangle\,\blacktriangle$

ON AVERAGE, SERVICEMEN and women relocate every two years. However, during my tour of duty in Vietnam, I was on the move constantly, from one mission or operation to another. Little did I know that this unrest would settle deep into my psyche and consequently, I would move often even after I left the war behind. Although it would take more than ten years after I left Vietnam before PTSD was added into the American Psychiatric Association Manual, its symptoms were becoming more and more pronounced in my behavior.

For the next ten years following my discharge from the U.S. Marine Corps, I made seven different moves, relocating from state to state, job to job. To start, along with my discharge certificate, I received an airline ticket to my next destination. My first location after Camp Pendleton, was Bridgeport, Connecticut, where Mama, my sister, Alice, and some of my uncles were now living. Upon my arrival, Uncle Carl allowed me to move in with him while I searched for my own apartment.

My first order of business was apartment and job hunting through the local newspaper. Following those tasks, I focused on reading and learning about world events. Articles about the ongoing war in Vietnam really angered me and left me feeling depressed. It saddened me to know that youngsters averaging the age of nineteen could go to a distant land and fight a war that they didn't really understand, only to return stateside and be called "baby killers," In reality we were honorable patriotic soldiers of war, following orders of our U.S. commanders. One such article depicted soldiers of the Vietnam War as drug addicts. I can't defend or deny those allegations. Perhaps some soldiers did indulge in drugs, but certainly not the marines from Unit 2/4. We were too damn busy in the bush, fighting the enemy and covering our asses to stay alive.

I also read an article about a grandmother who lost her grandson in the Vietnam War. In her moment of grief, she'd gone to the airport and shot one of the veterans as he exited the plane. It was disappointing and heartbreaking to learn that there were people in the world who thought like that. The grandmother made a choice to kill someone. Being soldiers, we didn't make killing a choice. We were soldiers obeying our command.

⋀ ⋀ ⋀

On the flip side, my military service had its privileges when it came to job hunting. I never had a problem obtaining a good job. My only problem was keeping a job once I got it. There was still that restlessness working against me that kept me on the move, just like during the war. It was the PTSD.

For my first job in Connecticut, I was hired at Avco Lycoming Division which made parts for ship engines. It was a factory job of sorts which I quickly learned to dislike. I lasted as long as I could, which was about a year, then resigned, on the spot.

My next job in Connecticut was at General Electric. I worked there in various positions for about a year. Although different from Avco, it was still a factory position. I liked the job well enough at first, but, I noticed this stirring within me urging me to move on. I also discovered something unique about myself, sort of a self-discovery moment. My next job would not be in a factory, as factory work was not my forte.

CHAPTER 27

———— ▲ ▲ ▲ ————

ASIDE FROM WORKING through the week on a job I didn't particularly like, I would escape on the weekends to the "Big Apple." The bright lights and shopping in China Town was just what I needed to revive me for the upcoming work week. I made a point to check out places like Times Square, Central Park, and the museums. I saw it all! With a different pretty girl hanging on my arm, we'd dine at a nice restaurant and then hit the Apollo in Harlem to watch the various artists perform.

My fascination with New York, was bittersweet. There were times when I enjoyed the euphoria like being on R & R from the war. At the same time, the constant movement of the subway, buses and taxi cabs, combined with the noises ignited a feeling of nostalgia for the action back in the war. New York, certainly kept me on full alert, just like Vietnam. There was something about the stress and the pleasure of it all that kept drawing me back. Now, I know it was the PTSD that was settling deep within. I just hadn't learned to identify and cope with it yet.

For a long time, I didn't allow anyone to get close enough to touch my heart, not the way Sandra had. I guess there's some truth to that *first* love experience which sets the criteria for what love is supposed to feel like.

Many times my thoughts returned to Brenda and the good times we shared in the Philippines. I often thought about taking that journey back to try and pick up where we left off, but for some reason, the long distance and the idea of working in the Philippines was not appealing.

When I finally did let down my guard, it was for a girl named Leeta. We were introduced by my sister, Alice, while I was still living in Connecticut. Leeta was a true beauty. Together, we were like fireballs. After a brief whirlwind of a courtship, we ended up engaged to be married. I really loved Leeta, but truthfully, I wasn't ready for a full commitment. I wanted nothing to hold me down, and I wanted to hold on to that freedom to go at a moment's notice.

The whole relationship with Leeta blew up after her mother's boyfriend saw me with one of my female friends. Truthfully, she was merely a friend, but the way he put it gave Leeta the impression that I was seeing another girl behind her back. I was so angry with him that I had thoughts of murder. I confronted him and a heated argument ensued. At the last minute, I flipped the butcher knife and using the handle instead of the blade, I struck *ol'* boy in the head. After the pandemonium, I looked back at what had just occurred as if I had gone through an out-of-body experience. I knew something was wrong with me, something *majorly* wrong. It was then that I decided it best to leave Bridgeport.

That night, my sleep was conflicted with nightmares of the war. Upon rising, I left town without saying goodbye to Leeta. That evening, I called Alice and pleaded with her not to tell Leeta my true whereabouts. I had made it to Cleveland, Ohio, feeling desperate for a new start.

CHAPTER 28

━━━ ▲▲▲ ━━━

EVEN AS A young girl, Viola admitted she always took notice of men in uniform. Working at the Cleveland Clinic, she'd seen plenty, mostly hospital staff and military soldiers in uniform. When she first laid eyes on me, I was sporting my hospital *whites* in my new position as an orderly. Viola was forthright when she said, "With good looks like yours, the type of uniform doesn't matter." She told me that I stand out in a crowd, and she wasn't the only one who noticed.

I didn't care how many women were taking notice. I had just made a fast exit out of Connecticut, leaving my heart behind with Leeta. Getting involved in a new relationship was the last thing on my mind. Nevertheless, sometimes the best things come to you when you're not looking for it. Unbeknownst to me, Viola first approached me as a dare, provoked by some of the nurses on 3 north. Turns out, the dare was worthwhile as she was easy to talk to and before I knew it, we became good friends.

As my friendship with Viola progressed, I found myself visiting her at her apartment after work. She had the most adorable kids, two boys and two girls: Twanda, age (7);

Maurice, age (6); Renese, age (4); and Kelvin was age (2). Almost immediately, I found myself getting attached to her children, all four of them, and I started to spend more and more time at Viola's.

Had it not been for Viola and her kids, I may have given in sooner than later to the stirring that always precipitated a change in my surroundings. This time, because of them, I tried to fight the urge and hung in there longer than I really wanted to.

Sheer exhaustion was the final straw that stretched me beyond the limit. As an orderly, my primary responsibility was to transport patients to and from various labs for testing. It was also my responsibility to transport dead bodies to the morgue. One of the perks was an opportunity to observe autopsies, which I found extremely interesting.

I'd been working at the hospital just over two years when things began to spiral down. The hospital had been short staffed and I had worked nine consecutive double shifts. Extreme exhaustion had set in. When I received my paycheck, a generous amount due to all the overtime, the urge to leave hit me, just like that. I called off sick and never went back.

CHAPTER 29

————— ▲ ▲ ▲ —————

THE UNITED STATES Marine Corps (USMC) recruiter wasted no time in processing my paperwork. American soldiers were still engaged in combat in Vietnam and that's exactly where he was planning to send me. Right back to the war. That was fine with me. In fact, it excited me like a kid with a brand new toy. I felt revived and ready to go. Truth was, I'd spent more than three years in the military before I returned to the world. Only I couldn't fit in. The only place I truly felt comfortable and had performed my best was during the war. In spite of my wounds, I wanted to return. It was funny how it occurred to me. Almost overnight, I had convinced myself that I wanted to make a career in the Marine Corps.

On November 7, 1973, I reported for duty at Marine Corps Recruit Depot (MCRD) San Clemente, California. Shortly thereafter, I sent for Viola. This was no hard decision for her. With temperatures in the low twenties in Cleveland, Ohio, she and the kids were more than ready for sunshiny, California.

For the first year, everything went smoothly with my training. Then suddenly, everything changed and my plans of making a career in the military came to a screeching halt. During one of the training exercises, it was noticed that my shoulders had been rebuilt. That discovery lead to a deeper investigation into my medical history. Back in Vietnam, my shoulder took a hit from a rocket. I didn't sustain a puncture wound, it was more of a strain or like a dislocated shoulder. Certainly not an injury that warranted a Purple Heart.

After I left Vietnam, there'd been times when I'd experience intermittent, thirty second, flare-ups in my shoulders. X-rays revealed nothing out of the ordinary. Still, there were times when I attempted to open a door, and turning the knob would send a pain searing straight through my shoulders.

While I was working as an orderly at the Cleveland Clinic, a new procedure was introduced. The procedure involved transferring ligaments from top to bottom and inserting fiberglass screws, first in my right shoulder and then my left. The end results were two rebuilt shoulders. The surgery was a success and the pain soon dissipated. Thus, I considered myself cured.

I was really looking forward to returning to combat, something that I had long missed, but unfortunately, that would not be the case. I was discharged, for the second time in, 1973, blaming my shoulders for bringing my newfound dream of a career in the U.S. Marine Corps to an abrupt end.

After my second honorable discharge from the Marine Corps, Viola and I decided to stay in California. During this time, I took her shopping for a ring. Once we made our selection, I proposed right there in the jewelry store. We were married on January 17, 1974, in a small chapel with the minister and his wife as witnesses.

▲ ▲ ▲

Our entire family enjoyed living in San Clemente, California. It rarely rained and the mild temperatures allowed us to enjoy numerous outdoor activities with the kids. They especially enjoyed making lemonade fresh from the lemons that grew on a tree in our own backyard.

▲ ▲ ▲

When Viola and I left California, it wasn't that we sat down and made plans to leave. The decision sort of evolved following an incident involving our neighbor who was being harassed by two neighborhood bullies. I guess the "combat" still within me caused me to fester about it, and one evening I laid in wait for a glimpse of the two thugs. It didn't take long before the opportunity presented itself and I confronted them. Fortunately for them and for me, Viola came to the rescue and pleaded with me to stop. Had she not been there to stop me short of pulling my trigger, I might have spent some time in prison. Shortly after that altercation, we pulled up stakes leaving a house filled with furniture behind. We then hit the highway heading to Bridgeport, Connecticut. Mama was sick and in the hospital at the time, and I wanted to go and be close to her for a while.

▲ ▲ ▲

During my visit with Mama, we reminisced about the past and she surprised me with a box that she'd labeled, "Jerry." Its contents included letters I had sent her from Vietnam, my sweater from high school, my birth certificate, and various trophies awarded from my high school sports. Our visit was filled with nostalgia that did wonders for my bruised spirit.

I also had a visit with my Uncle Alonzo who convinced me to go to the Veterans Clinic. He was concerned about the rash on my hands and he'd noticed that my happy-go-lucky demeanor had been replaced with anger. It seemed like everyone was glaring at me and for some odd reason, it stirred up feelings of guilt. Guilty of what, I'm not sure I can explain. As a result, I'd snap, "What you looking at?"

The veteran's hospital was located in West Haven, Connecticut. Within minutes, the doctor diagnosed the rash, on both my hands and feet, as jungle rot. The rash was not causing me any real pain, but it itched like hell and the various creams that I'd applied since leaving Vietnam had only provided temporary relief. The doctor had seen jungle rot often on soldiers.With the high temperatures in Vietnam and constant moisture in my boots, it was almost inevitable that I'd develop it. I was really glad that I listened to Uncle Alonzo for the prescriptive cream helped, tremendously.

As for the discussion with the doctor about my anger, he prescribed a drug with some serious side effects. PTSD was not yet named as a disorder, so there was no therapist offering group therapy, just a drug so potent it knocked me out. The way the doctor treated me, I felt like a specimen. I didn't enjoy his bedside manner, or lack thereof. I especially didn't enjoy the effects of the drugs he prescribed. Needless to say, I refused to schedule any follow-up visits.

▲▲▲

Agent Orange was also scaring the hell out of everybody in the '70s. Both American and Vietnamese veterans and their families have suffered many years as a result of the toxic chemicals that was sprayed over the agricultural land by the U.S. military. Birth defects, cancer, myeloma, Hodgkin's disease and other medical issues have been listed as dire consequences.

Agent Orange was intended as a warfare program to kill the brush and foliage where the enemy hid so well. It was sprayed over Vietnam from 1961, through the early '70s, before it was finally banned by the Environmental Protection

Agency. Being that I was a marine directly exposed to the chemical during the Vietnam War, I became a recipient of the class action lawsuit settlement.

▲ ▲ ▲

My family and I spent about two weeks in Bridgeport. Mama was doing better and was busy making plans to move again. This time, she and Alice would be moving in different directions. Mama was moving on to Cleveland, Ohio, to live with her daughter, Jean and her children. Alice wanted to be near our mother, Cora Mae, so she moved to Warren, Ohio, where she resided until she passed away from a heart attack in 2013.

About the same time, Mama moved to Cleveland, Ohio, Viola and I decided to move on to Muncie, Indiana, to be near her family.

▲ ▲ ▲

When we arrived in Muncie, we stayed with Viola's family for a brief time while we searched for our own place. Before too long, we found the Chateau Apartments. Incidentally, we were the first blacks to live at the Chateau. To move in, I needed $1100 for the deposit of which I did not have. After mulling it over, I swallowed my pride and went to my father-in-law, Viola's father, Dave. "When I get my first check from my VA benefits, I *will* repay you," I promised.

"That's fine with me, son. Now, if for some reason you don't receive your check like you expect, give me a call and let me know. Don't just ignore me now. Make me understand your story."

I was so grateful to Dave and true to my word, when I received my first VA check, I repaid my debt. "Thank you, Dave. Here's your money, and I won't ever borrow from you again," I said as I counted out his money.

"Never say never, son. Since you were good to your word, you can always come back to me." I hated to borrow money, but I really appreciated that my father-in-law and I had developed that level of trust between us.

▲ ▲ ▲

During our stay in Muncie, I took advantage of the GI bill which provided educational assistance to military servicemen and women. I enrolled in a radio/TV school and also studied industrial electronics. I attended school during the day and Viola worked the night shift as a nurse aide at Ball Memorial Hospital.

▲ ▲ ▲

On December 18, 1975, Viola gave birth to our son, Jerry, making us the proud parents of our first child together. Now we had a total of five children to raise. Nothing like the fifteen that Mama and Daddy had raised, but we had a houseful, just the same.

We stayed in Muncie for about a year before we decided to move on. With baby Jerry still in diapers, Viola and I loaded up all the kids into our antique '53 Cadillac, Fleetwood.

I had ditched the Chevy for the Caddy, since a much larger vehicle was needed to accommodate our family, especially for all of our moves. That baby was a tank! Twice I was hit from the rear and both times the damage was to the other car. My Caddy only sustained a couple of hair scratches. At this time, something was urging me to be near my biological father, James Small, so we took off heading for Columbus, Ohio.

In Columbus, Ohio, I continued to utilize the GI bill by pursuing my education at Bell & Howell's, TV/Radio repair school. I really did have a knack for fixing broken TVs and radios. It was gratifying taking them apart and putting them back together again. For some reason though, I wasn't totally satisfied that fixing small electronics was my one and only calling. I'd also been impressed with the medics during my short stints in the hospital in Vietnam, and I truly appreciated all they did for the other soldiers and me. If I could give back, even in a small way, I thought that would give me a greater sense of purpose. Just like that, I made a drastic switch from fixing small electronics to pursuing my newfound desire to assist mankind with their health issues. I knew I didn't have the stamina to stay put for a decade in medical school, but the nursing program offered at the Ohio Institute of Technology (OIT) was something I thought I could handle. I attended the courses for about a year before I decided it was time to move on.

Had the VA not paid for my training, perhaps I would have settled into a profession much sooner than I did, but the educational funds were endless and fortunately for me, so were my varied interests. Still, even after being trained in radio/TVs and nursing, I didn't find any interesting long term jobs in Columbus. I remember thinking that I needed to settle down, but my PTSD made it hard to be still. I needed to be on the go, like in the war, moving from one place to another.

CHAPTER 30

▲ ▲ ▲

DURING THE SPRING of 1978, I gave in to the urge to move my family once again. This time, we moved from Columbus, Ohio, to Kalamazoo, Michigan, to be near my Uncle Carl who had also relocated to Kalamazoo, from Connecticut.

Perhaps it was the beginning of spring. The start of new things like plants and flowers sprouting from the earth, like buds that laid dormant through the winter starting to grow again, like birds migrating north. All these mark the beginning of spring, but for the Williams family, the spring of 1978, represented a new city, new job, and a new home. For the first time, I experienced a true feeling of permanence in the air. In fact, the first house that I ever wanted to buy was located in Kalamazoo. I'd been driving along a couple streets over from the apartment we were renting, when I came upon the perfect house on the perfect street, "Williams Street." The house was exceptionally nice with a fireplace, fenced in yard and wide front porch. And, with the street name coinciding with my last name, it had to be an omen. A good omen. I was certainly willing to believe that my Divine Creator had guided me to that house on Williams Street as a sign to settle down. And that's what I intended to do.

I was eligible for a VA home loan, but I needed additional income and hadn't yet found a job. When the realtor, a white man, learned that I was a veteran, he went above and beyond to help me. First, he recommended that I be interviewed at the Kalamazoo Water Treatment Plant. Immediately following the interview, I was offered the position of waste water treatment operator. The second thing he did, which I would have given up without his help, was assist me step by step with the mounds of documents needed to process the loan. Before too long, Viola and I, and our five kids had moved in, proud owners of our very first home located on Williams Street.

The kids liked their new house, new friends and even their new school where they were excelling in all their classes. I believe they too could feel Kalamazoo was home, unlike some of our former residences.

Viola surrounded by her five children

I didn't realize how tough it had been on the kids. No sense of stability due to the constant moving, from place to place. As soon as they'd make new friends, they'd be rooted up and moved again. It was difficult for them having to adjust every time we moved. Of course I didn't realize it at the time.

Viola was very happy with the house. She spent the first year or so decorating and being a stay at home mom. Eventually, she went to work at the Brunson Hospital in Kalamazoo.

▲ ▲ ▲

I hit the ground running in my new position at the Kalamazoo Water Treatment Plant. I was trained to drive a dump truck, learned to use waste water treatment chemicals to recycle water, and monitored chemical readings to determine bacterial counts to purify the city's water. With the wide variety of responsibilities, I never got bored, and I actually looked forward to going to work each day.

About two years into the job, I was on the second leg of a double shift when the alarms began in the incinerator room. It had been my responsibility to monitor the meters and deposit chemicals when necessary. Suddenly, the alarms began indicating that the shaft had been blocked. To unblock it, and stop the shaft from going any further, I had to open the incinerator door and place the switch on neutral. I proceeded to stick a bar in the door to hold it open. Once I observed the blockage, I used a large iron bar to push the blockage out of the way. Unfortunately, the neutral switch didn't hold. I was truly blessed that only my ear was cut, for it really could have been my entire head. I felt no sharp pain - it just felt more like a fifty pound weight sitting on top of my head. With no memory of it, I walked back into the plant with clipboard in hand and bleeding like a hog. My ear was severely cut and hanging half way down close to my neck. When the supervisor responded to the alarms sounding off, he noticed a trail of blood and followed it back to the main office. I remember someone yelled, "Call an ambulance!"

Within minutes, I was on a stretcher being rushed to a waiting ambulance. My current situation, however, was abruptly interrupted and I was back in the war zone of Vietnam being carted off to a waiting chopper. The paramedics reported that I was obviously experiencing a flashback for I was yelling, "Lieutenant Shortenton, Lieutenant Shortenton."

I was indeed blessed to be at the right place at the right time, as one of the leading plastic surgeons was on duty in the ER. He performed the surgery and reattached my left ear. In addition to my severed ear, I had suffered a concussion.

In the aftermath following my surgery, a nurse helped me sort out the flashbacks. The alarms sounding off, indicating the emergency inside the water plant, had triggered the flashbacks of rockets and gunfire noise in Vietnam. The injury to my ear mimicked my wound in action. This explanation seemed simple enough to understand and even normal following a concussion, but in reality the freaky accident with my ear was the turning point that prompted many PTSD symptoms to rise to the surface. First, I began fighting the urge to take flight again and make a new start. For this feeling to surface again considering my strong attachment to Kalamazoo and our new home, was confusing as hell to me. After all, I had come to think of our home on Williams Street as our forever home. In addition, I continued to have flashbacks and nightmares about Vietnam. Eventually, it occurred to me that being at the water plant was a constant reminder of my traumatic ear accident, and therefore, the plant *had* to be the source of my flashbacks. Consequently, I resigned from the water plant.

▲ ▲ ▲

Once again, I made a visit to the VA and began using my GI bill. This time, I registered to study business administration at the Davenport Business College in Kalamazoo. This decision turned into a very positive experience, but in other areas of my life, the symptoms of PTSD were becoming more and more evident. Nightmares interrupted my sleep at night and mood swings were a constant source of tension between Viola and me. I tried to keep my mind focused on repairing TVs and my school work, but as time went by, things got worse. As the tension mounted, I convinced myself that Viola and the kids would be better off without me. One day, when I thought I couldn't take it anymore, I picked up the phone and called my Uncle Ferbee.

A couple days later, I boarded the Greyhound, and a few hours later, Uncle Ferbee picked me up at the station in downtown Cleveland, Ohio.

CHAPTER 31

— ▲ ▲ ▲ —

FINDING A NEW job was always fast and easy for me. I had only been back in Cleveland a few days when I heard about the grand opening of Sun TV, a home appliance chain out of Columbus, Ohio. With my prior training and passion for electronics, I was hired immediately following the interview, as a TV salesman.

With the grand opening underway, there was no shortage of customers. I was busy learning the products and helping the customers make decisions about their purchases. I was feeling good.

The first problem began when my first paycheck didn't arrive on the truck from Columbus. It arrived two days late. I was pissed, but managed to keep it together.

Just when I was getting back into the swing of things, the same thing happened with the next paycheck. This time I acted out and threatened the manager. "When them trucks come in next Thursday and them checks are not on it, I'm going to have my pistol and take *your* money." They obviously took my threat seriously, for the next week the checks were delivered on time. Subsequently, with my check in hand, I was given my walking papers. That was the first and only time I've ever been fired from any job. I didn't resist, but I swore, Sun TV would never get a penny from me as a future customer. With my passion for TVs, they'd certainly lose out on plenty of my money.

▲ ▲ ▲

Following the disaster at Sun TV, I decided to pick up where I left off with my business courses. Little did I know that Mr. Long, the service agent who handled my educational benefits at the Davenport Business School, had also left Kalamazoo and was now working at the Cleveland Regional Federal Building. How ironic that he'd begin handling my education benefits in Cleveland, just like he had in Kalamazoo. It was Mr. Long's recommendation that I go through the VA's vocational rehab program which just happened to have an opening as a clerk in the federal building. "This will be a great opportunity to get your foot in the door," said Mr. Long. "Do a good job and perhaps you'll be hired on when a permanent General Schedule (GS) position becomes available."

"Sure, no problem." It was never a problem for me to find a job and I didn't mind going to work each day. "I'm on my way."

As I left Mr. Long's office, that "new beginning" feeling stirred within me. I was especially excited about the possibilities of this new career path as it would lead to a GS position which referred to white collar status within the federal government system. Perhaps now, I could leave behind those warehouse and industrial type jobs, which were never my forte.

▲ ▲ ▲

The line of communication was always open between Viola and me and our kids. Still, I was missing my family like crazy. Although it was hard to give up the house we all loved so much on Williams Street, I returned to Kalamazoo, packed up Viola and the kids and brought them back to Cleveland with me.

The first time Viola and I left Cleveland, it was 1972. By way of California, Connecticut, Indiana, Ohio, and Michigan, we were now returning, having come full circle, back to Cleveland. The year was now 1980.

I also felt good about being in Cleveland near Mama again. Her health had been failing and she was now in a nursing home. Being close in vicinity gave me the opportunity to visit her more often. Mama passed away in 1981, at the age of 87.

CHAPTER 32

———— ▲ ▲ ▲ ————

WITH MY FAMILY all together again in Cleveland, Viola and I began a lengthy search for a house, similar to the one we had just vacated in Kalamazoo. We wanted a home that we all could love again. We lucked up when we found a two-story house on the southeast side of Cleveland, close to Shaker Heights. We started out renting with the option to buy after two years.

During those first two years, our payments were made timely, so I was quite perplexed and annoyed when letters began to arrive from Countrywide Mortgage, threatening to foreclose. Determined not to lose my house, I called my friend, Amos Simmons, who worked at the federal building. Amos introduced me to an attorney who declined because he didn't handle those type of cases. That lawyer was kind enough to refer me to George Penfield, another lawyer within the firm. Ironically, George's wife, Victoria, was a podiatrist who treated a number of veterans at the VA with their foot ailments.

Fortunately, Attorney George Penfield took my case *pro bono* and exposed the sleazy con artist who I'd been paying rent to for two years. Unfortunately, the foreclosure went forward as the mortgage company planned, and my home was scheduled for auction. I felt terrible, but I was a marine and wasn't ready to give up. Thankfully, George had a back-up plan, and so did I.

A few days before my house was scheduled for auction at the sheriff's sale, I decided to parade on my front lawn dressed in my Marine Corps combat gear. My hope was to deter any prospective buyers who might drive by for an advance look at my property and to let them know that I wasn't giving up without a fight.

For the sheriff's sale, the bidding process required 10% down in cash, with the remainder due within thirty days. Although I was prepared to purchase my house from the auction, I wasn't prepared to accept that the bank representative had outbid me. I was devastated.

Three days before Christmas, as my family was on the verge of packing up to vacate our house in defeat, a Channel 3 TV news reporter, Tom Beres, knocked on my door. With cameras rolling, I told Tom my story.

Later that evening, the news anchor announced, "Vietnam vet thought he was doing the right thing, but was being conned." I will never forget Tom Beres - nice man with a real heart for humanity.

Although previous attempts had been made to reach Countrywide Mortgage, they had made zero attempts to re-spond. Not until the presentation was televised. A few days later, a representative not only called, but arrived in the flesh from Texas and rewrote the loan for me. I can hardly express the relief and gratitude I felt towards George and

Tom for their efforts in saving my home. Throughout that sordid lengthy ordeal, George and I crossed the line of attorney and client, and became good friends.

▲ ▲ ▲

I wish I could say that the snafu with Countrywide Mortgage was the first and only attempt to take my house from me. Unfortunately, another attempt was made a couple years later. This time, the perpetrator was a fellow veteran, whom I met at the VA.

Like most friendships, things started out kinda cool between M.C. and me. Actually, more than cool when you consider he invited me on a trip to Punta Cana in the Dominican Republic. Originally M.C. and his wife had planned to vacation at a five star hotel along the Atlantic Ocean, but about a week or so before the trip, M.C.'s wife couldn't go and he asked me to join him on the all expense paid trip. I'd never been anywhere close to Punta Cana, so I accepted and packed my bags. We had a blast at the all inclusive resort, and needless to say, our friendship grew. M.C. sort of reminded me of Lieutenant Shortenton and I found myself trusting him.

I don't know how long M.C. had been planning his scam, but when he asked me to sign my name on a legal document, he spun it so that I thought I was helping him out of a situation. I guess I had been around my attorney, George, long enough to smell something odd about this, or at least, I needed a second opinion.

The following day, I rushed over to George's office and slapped the document on his desk. "Does this look legit to you?"

"Sit down and let me look it over." Within a few minutes, George was on the phone making calls to correct the situation. It was a total shock to my system to learn that I had signed a document turning over my house to M.C. It was also devastating to learn that I had put my trust in the wrong man. Another veteran at that! I operate on the principle to help a veteran, however I can. Never hurt a veteran. I was crushed that M.C. would treat me like that and needless to say, my trust issues intensified.

At the VA, I informed my therapist and doctor about M.C.'s attempt to scam me. To my surprise, both admitted it was a psychological set-up. I felt that I had made myself vulnerable to M.C. for he knew me as having PTSD and thought he could take advantage of me. Again, and again, I am grateful to have George in my life to review matters for me.

▲ ▲ ▲

Over the years, my friendship with George continued to grow, and I found myself sharing practically all of my concerns in other areas of my life. Even when I didn't know it, George's vast legal knowledge spotted potential pitfalls that he offered to handle for me. Banking and financial matters was a major challenge for me and more than once, George interceded and straightened things out. I was always grateful. George didn't charge me for his services, but in return, I handled various home repairs and other small jobs for him and Victoria.

I would highly recommend anyone with PTSD to find someone trustworthy and qualified to help manage all financial matters.

CHAPTER 33

— ▲ ▲ ▲ —

It was a typical busy Monday at the federal building where I had now been employed for five years. Things had been going extremely well. I began as a clerk through the VA's vocational rehab program, then applied for the loan guarantee position. I then interviewed with Stewart MacArthur (Mac) and was instructed on how to study for the civil service exam. As it turned out, MacArthur and Coach Starlings had gone to college together.

I studied for the civil service exam and passed. Of course, I was extremely grateful for the additional points that were added to my score for being a veteran, and even more points were added for being a wounded veteran.

In my new position as a loan guarantee clerk, a GS employee, I handled the paperwork for veterans who were on the verge of losing their homes due to foreclosure. In time, I learned the entire process, including a veteran's right to appeal in an effort to save their homes. It was a very rewarding position and that dreadful urging that usually appeared after a year or so on the job hadn't surfaced in five years. This marked a huge milestone for me.

My dress attire consisted of a suit and tie, and I even carried a briefcase, compliments of the vocational rehab program. I had a respectable position that I felt my children could speak about with pride.

Janelle, a processing officer, appeared at my cubicle and made a sarcastic announcement. "That Mr. Little is at the front desk asking for you. Again!" she emphasized with unmistakable attitude.

Cleon Little had showed up at the federal building three times previously seeking my assistance. This time, he had his wife in tow. It seemed every time he made one step of progress in the process of saving his home, he'd hit a snag. One snag after another. I felt bad for his inconvenience and tried my best to help. After all, he'd been a corporal, a fellow Marine, who had served our country for six years before receiving a medical discharge.

As I stood at the counter explaining the process to Mr. Little and his wife, I was acutely aware of Janelle who was nice enough to my face, but always pulling her round rim glasses down over her nose and looking over her shoulder at me. I guess in every office, the boundary between employee and customer had to be honored. But, with Mr. Little, I found myself stepping into that gray area - going *over and beyond* the call of duty.

The following day, Mac called me into his office. "Have a seat."

I obliged and sat back in the hard narrow chair across from Mac's desk, with no idea of what was to come. In an

accusatory tone, he started in. "Herman, can you explain why
Mr. Little has been to this office four times asking for you?"

That damn Janelle, I knew she'd been waiting for an opportunity to stab me in the back. "Sure, Mac. No problem.
It seems like Mr. Little is experiencing one snag after another, and I was simply explaining the process and assisting
him with his paperwork."

"Well actually, it is a problem. Haven't you been warned,
let's see," Mac looked down and searched through the pile of
documents on his desk. "Several times you've been warned
against fraternizing with the veterans and going outside the
scope of your job duties. Now, you've been warned about
this before. Am I right?"

It was true. Word of mouth had spread far and wide that
if you needed help with your VA paperwork, I was the man
to see. Because of the many friends I'd lost in the war and
because of the veterans who never made it back, it became
natural for me to do all I could to help a veteran. It was also
my opinion that I stayed within the boundaries of government policy, so I wasn't jeopardizing anything. As a result,
more and more veterans were showing up requesting my
help. "Yes sir, you are right. What's the big deal? I've always
received good evaluations and the feedback from the veterans who took the time to write back about my assistance has
always been good."

"It is a big deal," Mac interrupted. "If this was a retail
establishment, you'd be accused of giving away the store.
You can't do that, Herman."

Within minutes, the exchange between Mac and me escalated. I had always respected him, and I felt the respect was mutual. Now, however, my anger was on the rise.

Sometimes you make a choice to go right, and along the way, you give your absolute best. Your good and loyal service helps a few, then suddenly, a detour brings that service to a dead end. Sitting across from Mac, I realized I had reached that crossroads. I could either go left, against my natural grain, or simply leave. For me, it was do or die.

Numb, I exited the federal building. As I walked to my car, my temper was starting to boil and thoughts of destruction began to fill my head. It took a few days before my anger simmered down. I was thankful that my discipline, instilled as a marine, had remained steady. Had my anger erupted, I could have ended up behind bars, incarcerated for life, and missed the opportunity of meeting Dr. Jorge.

At the Veterans Care Center on Cleveland's west side, I met with Dr. Jorge and admitted that I was in dire need of help. Our meeting lasted two hours after which he directed me to the Veterans Administration Medical Center in Brecksville, to be screened for Post Traumatic Stress Disorder, PTSD. As Dr. Jorge pointed out, PTSD, according to the National Center for PTSD, is a mental health problem that some develop after experiencing a life threatening event such as combat, natural disaster, car accident or sexual assault. "Please don't be ashamed of that and take the right step to treatment," he pleaded with me.

Viola was genuinely happy that I was considering the program. After all, she and the kids had taken a lot, especially during the months between November to January, my worst times. According to Viola and the kids, my mood swings were frequent and at least twice, she had taken me to the hospital following an outburst of anger, ranting and raving, swearing and throwing things.

CHAPTER 34

— ▲ ▲ ▲ —

ON A SUNNY Monday morning in June, 1989, I drove myself to the huge Veterans Administration (VA) Medical Center, located south of Cleveland, in an upscale community known as Brecksville, Ohio. I was in awe of the beautiful lush green manicured grounds with pavilions and ponds, tucked away on fifty acres, away from the hustle and bustle of the city. The drug free environment felt safe. It included a large PX military exchange store, softball field, bowling alley, movie theater, a state of the art fitness center, and a barbershop. Everything anyone needed to recover in a safe and secure environment was here, including a chapel.

Veterans participating in the PTSD program were housed in the Center for Stress Recovery (CSR) which was located in the domiciliary of the hospital along with the homeless and disabled veterans. We were kept separate from everyone else because we have a hard time sleeping and frequently sit up all hours of the night talking in the television room.

Another veteran andI shared an assigned room containing two twin size beds with a trundle drawer to store a few items of clothing and personal belongings. We shared a book case for a small stereo. We were both paranoid enough to believe that a speaker must have been hidden inside the wall for the doctors to listen in on us. Finally, taped to the inside door of our room was a list of PTSD symptoms. The list was hand written, so I assumed the author was a former veteran who occupied the room, previously.

SYMPTOMS OF PTSD

1. **Recurring thoughts while awake**
2. **Recurring nightmares**
3. **Sleepless nights**
4. **Feelings of guilt**
5. **Mood swings**
6. **Increased distress approaching an anniversary of a traumatic event**
7. **Road rage**
8. **Excessive Profanity**

When I reached the bottom of the list, I started again at the top. This time, I focused long and hard on each symptom. As I began to comprehend the full impact of PTSD and the damage it had done to me *and* my family, I became overwhelmed. Memories began to unfold as past violent episodes took center stage in my mind. I replayed my behavior during a Thanksgiving dinner held at our home in Cleveland. My whole family had been seated around the table, including my mother, Cora Mae, who had made a rare visit to share the holiday with us. The food was exceptional, the adult conversation was light and cheerful and my grandchildren were playing well together. Everything was going along just perfect until I witnessed my seven year old grandson hit my thirteen year old son with a plastic sword. In retaliation, my son grabbed the sword and snapped it in two. Next thing I know, they were holding me back. I never liked to see children getting hurt and whenever I'd witness parents berating or chastising their own children, no matter if they needed it, I'd lose control, just snap. For the life of me, I can't remember my actions. I do recall tears rolling down my son's face, and family members ushering their children out the door in a hurry. Items once nailed to the walls were now in heaps of broken wood and glass on the floor. I had ruined a perfectly good Thanksgiving dinner.

Thanks to Viola's nursing experience, she instantly recognized that I needed immediate attention and quickly ushered me out of the house and to the hospital. Oddly, by the time we arrived, my anger had vanished, and I was calm again.

Regarding the mental consequences of my behavior, I'll never really know how deeply my family was affected. The children shuddered when I dared to approach the subject later, so needless to say, speaking of the incident is taboo in the Williams' household. Remembering this long ago episode still brings a sadness to my heart.

On another occasion while driving through Newburg Heights, a cop from the NHPD turned on his lights and pulled me over. I don't recall the reason, but it was trivial and angered me to the point that I exchanged angry words with the cop. The kids seated in the back were afraid for me and began yelling out, "Don't, Dad, don't, Dad!" When the officer ran my driver's license, he learned that due to my condition, I was not to be arrested. Instead, I should be transported to a VA medical center, if it becme necessary. Road rage was a common occurrence for me, as well as other PTSD victims. That time, the officer let me go with a warning.

From the list of symptoms written on the back of my door, I had experienced them all.

One of the worst feelings about having PTSD is realizing its damage to my family. Having reoccurring nightmares about the things I saw during the war is to be expected. But, when I realized my PTSD had caused me to rob my family of a better quality of life, and that they too had suffered as a result of my PTSD, I had to wonder if I had been a blessing or a curse to Viola and her kids. I desperately wanted to make it up to them.

With no possible way to turn back the hands of time, I resigned to do the next best thing which was to be serious about my treatment and recovery. I could only hope that in time, my family would come to understand and forgive me for my actions which were the consequences of being a victim of PTSD.

Three times a day, Monday through Friday, we attended group therapy sessions. I listened to other veterans as they poured out their traumatic experiences. Sharing was encouraged only after a veteran felt comfortable. I was still debating.

During one group exercise, we were tasked with writing down emotions like anger, shame and fear, followed by a full description of each emotion and how it felt. The objective of this exercise was to replace something negative with something positive. The feedback would be used as a model for future research in therapies.

During another group exercise, our therapist walked in wearing black pajamas. Wow, what a shock to the system! The pjs were similar to the uniforms worn by the enemy in Vietnam. Thoughts of the war came rushing back with a vengeance. Seeing those black pajamas again truly did evoke some disturbing emotions that the group had to spend quite a bit of time to process.

▲ ▲ ▲

After my second week at CSR, Viola came to visit. Spouses were permitted to attend some of the sessions, but her demanding work schedule didn't allow it. I had all kinds of mixed emotions and found it difficult to explain to Viola about the sorrow I felt for the pain I'd caused our family. At the same time, I was filled with hope that I'd found help in time and one day, I'd be able to show them by learning to cope with PTSD.

Having experience in nursing, Viola had empathy which combined with her love for me, equaled patience. That fact has been proven as we are still maintaining after forty one years.

"I'm glad you're here," she said after several awkward minutes. "Numerous nightmares, the mood swings and violent outbursts, you owe it to our family to find a better way to cope with your traumas."

Some nightmares were mild, then there were other intense nightmares with arms waving and feet kicking. Of course I've never witnessed these things, but as told by my wife, she describes my eyes being closed along with incoherent mumblings and utterings pouring from my mouth.

"I'm going to make it up to you and our kids. I promise."

"And how do you plan to make it up to us, Jerry?"

"For starters, I'm going to be serious about my treatment and recovery. And, after I've completed the program, I'm taking you on a lavish vacation." She smiled and nodded.

"Sounds good. But, you'd better be serious, Jerry."

▲ ▲ ▲

Throughout the following weeks of treatment at the CSR, I participated in various leisure time activities such as Bingo, a bus trip to a Cleveland Browns game, and local museums in downtown, Cleveland. The purpose of these type of trips was to allow my brain to experience positive things as opposed to those trauma related thoughts related to the fog of war.

Therapy also consisted of out of state field trips. Dr. Leibling believed the only way to get through a trauma is to confront it. Of course it wasn't feasible to travel back to Vietnam, but closer to home were Chinese restaurants which on my own, I totally avoided. Being a crucial component of my therapy, however, I was able to tolerate the shrimp fried rice, and eventually, I learned to overcome my distrust for the cooks preparing the meals. As time went by, I also learned to block out those ill feelings about Asians.

Another activity that served as a trigger of Vietnam was a bus trip to Washington, D.C., to visit the Vietnam Veterans Memorial Wall. I knew this trip would be hard for me, but still I looked forward to it. I walked slowly searching high and low for familiar names, particularly, Lieutenant Shortenton. I actually felt my shoulders tense as I braced myself for any display of emotion. After minutes of searching, Lieutenant Shortenton's name appeared. Seeing my Lieutenant's name on that wall was truly surreal. Although Dr. Leibling and a couple other veterans were nearby, they suddenly seemed like they were about fifty yards away. As I stepped closer, giving in to the temptation to touch the wall, I saw my own reflection looking back at me. I suddenly went numb. Dr. Leibling was observing my reaction and began closing the gap between us. "Herman, are you alright?" he asked. I nodded and my current reality resumed.

Herman standing in front of the Vietnam Vets Memorial Wall

Reliving those moments at the Memorial Wall keeps me going. It's that undisputable feeling of respect and honor for the dead. I can feel through their spirit that they're proud of me and wish me well in my pursuit to cope with my trauma and live a respectable life that they themselves were cut short of.

The group also took a bus tour to Gettysburg National Military Park in Gettysburg, Pennsylvania. Following each field trip, our therapist would help us process our feelings back at the treatment center.

If having PTSD wasn't already bad enough, imagine how I felt when I learned my family was subject to second hand PTSD. Immediately, after learning about this possibility, fear set in my bones that one or more of my kids might have contacted PTSD from me. Of the five kids, only one has displayed some minor tendencies.

CHAPTER 35

———— ▲ ▲ ▲ ————

IN INTERVALS OF every two weeks, I was allowed to leave CSR for the weekend and return on Sunday evening. It was also procedure, that on the Monday following a weekend out, I'd be required to undergo a urinalysis. One weekend I left the center and caught up with some friends of mine. Smoking marijuana was a common activity among this group of friends, but on this occasion, they were experimenting with some cocaine, as well. Eventually, I caved under the peer pressure to try it. Knowing that a marijuana joint by itself would not return a dirty urine, I proceeded to sprinkle only a tiny amount of the white powder onto my joint.

On the Monday after my experimental weekend, I submitted to the urinalysis. Shortly afterwards, I received a call from my therapist, Anita, asking me to come to her office. In a quiet tone, she explained. "Herman, your urine has turned up dirty." Before I could even think of a response, she went on. "It is strongly recommended that you participate in the four week program at VORK, that's the Veterans Addiction Rehabilitation Center."

I'm sure Anita had plenty of experience with other veterans in denial, as she was totally prepared for my outburst. "What? Just like that?"

"Listen," she started with authority. "It was explained to you, and I was very clear that you must remain clean and sober for 60 days prior to being accepted into the program. There's no way to pursue the traumatic material of this program if you're still using. Now, tell me you don't remember that?"

Even though I knew I was guilty, for some odd reason, I felt betrayed. Suddenly my anger rose and I began mouthing off to Anita.

"You can come back after VORK." she said, attempting to offer me some hope for the future.

I was too angry to accept her offer, and I stormed out of her office yelling, "I'm *never* coming back!"

I had failed to complete the program, and with that, I had failed my promise to Viola. Damn!

▲ ▲ ▲

Unlike the ward that housed veterans with PTSD, VORK was a rehab program for veterans with alcohol and substance abuse issues. Since my drug use was far from an addictive level, I didn't feel I was a candidate for the program. Nonetheless, the center had rules and I had no choice but to comply. Truth be told, I did learn some valuable information. During the four week program I learned to humble myself and listen. I learned that I didn't know everything even though I thought I did. I came to terms with my anger against Anita, realizing that it was my own wrongdoing that landed me at VORK, and I forgave her.

CHAPTER 36

— ▲ ▲ ▲ —

EVENTUALLY, I SIGNED up for another twelve week program. All in all, I have participated in the twelve week program four separate times. Not because I failed, but because I chose to. That's the wonderful part about therapy. Even though a veteran may show progress with his treatment, new traumas can develop and certain triggers can bring about unknown traumas. Just know that the psychotherapy will always be available for you, no matter how many times the need should arise.

When I entered the PTSD twelve week program for the *second* time, I was a model patient. I took part in treatments such as Intense Therapy, Warrior to Warrior, MAPP, RAP and more. One of my gains with therapy allowed for me to go to the movies and sit in the center of the theater without being paranoid that the enemy was lurking behind. Unfortunately, triggers from events like 9/11 and the more recent 2012, shootings in a Colorado movie theater can bring about old behaviors. It's alright to have those thoughts, but not alright to dwell on them. Therapy has taught me how to change my thought pattern whenever something traumatic happens.

Another gain allows me to shop at the local grocery store during the day, versus my 3:00 a.m. shopping sprees at the local Walmart stores. During the height of my PTSD, I'd try my best to avoid crowds like the plague. Now, I can shop during the day, but I don't linger. If a trigger arises, I quickly finish up my shopping and get the hell out of there.

Before watching television, I make a conscious effort to screen TV shows and movies in advance. I'm prone to have a nightmare if I watch a war flick or violent movie. If I have a nightmare, that means Viola's sleep is disrupted, so I have twice the reason to be careful about my selection of movies.

When learning to cope with PTSD symptoms, it's okay to have thoughts about my traumas, but not okay to act them out.

To promote creativity, there were many arts and crafts activities from which to choose. I enjoyed leather belt making, assembling model cars and more. Ceramics, however, became my favorite. In fact, I had become pretty darn good at making ceramic elephants and lighted nativity scenes. It felt good to work with my hands. I felt that *I* was being molded into something better than my current state. I also loved to read, and frequented the library for books on my favorite subjects such as history and science.

▲ ▲ ▲

With three good and healthy meals served each day at the CSR, a veteran may find themselves gaining weight. I picked up thirty pounds over the twelve weeks.

▲ ▲ ▲

Although I had listened to other veterans as they poured out their traumas during group session, it wasn't until the tenth week that I finally reached a level of comfort and began to share my own. One of my most courageous admissions was my guilt for Lt. Shortenton's death. Strangely, I didn't recall feeling guilty when it first happened during the Vietnam War, but years later I began to have flashbacks of my lieutenant's body lying exposed with his jaw and shoulders missing. My flashbacks were accompanied with an overwhelming feeling of uncertainty. I questioned myself over and over whether I was responsible for his death. Had it been my weapon that killed one of my most admired lieutenants? My guilt was surreal and painful. It was such a relief to learn that "guilt" is one of the demons of PTSD and "guilt" was experienced by other veterans in the group, as well.

I also shared with the group, my recurring nightmares which included images of a dead soldier stripped naked, with his penis cut off and stuffed in his mouth. Another vision, depicted a faded image of a soldier screaming in agony, "Lieutenant, what happened, what happened?" When the faded image came clear and in full view, the soldier would be me. The absolute worst recurring nightmare began with a soldier handing a dead baby, burned to a crisp, to its Vietnamese mother. My nightmares were complete with the scent of burning flesh and smoke which leaves me breathless for a few minutess upon awakening.

▲ ▲ ▲

At times, group sessions could become pretty intense. On one occasion, a veteran exploded in a fit of anger towards one of the therapist. Out of nowhere, he picked up a chair and threw it across the room. Within a flash, another chair went flying. By this point, I had developed a level of trust with our therapist, and wanted to protect her. I leaned into Sam, a veteran seated beside me, and whispered, "I'll go airborne if he sends another chair flying."

"And I'll go beneath," Sam replied.

Fortunately the therapist, being good at her job, was able to calm down the angry veteran.

▲ ▲ ▲

CHAPTER 37

I HAD MADE a promise to myself, to Viola and the therapists that I would take my recovery seriously. The other veterans noticed, as well. I didn't realize how much they'd noticed until they appointed me president of our unit. I was totally taken by surprise. In the role of president, veterans would come to me with issues, or suggestions to improve conditions at the center. I would then relay their concerns to the staff, but only if the issue was worthwhile. My fellow veterans knew that I was a no-nonsense guy, in spite of dealing with PTSD. Bogus matters had no merit with me.

▲ ▲ ▲

The promise I'd made to Viola about taking her on a lavish vacation materialized as a well-deserved hiatus for both of us following my twelve week program. Like many with PTSD, I had experienced occasional bouts where I felt unworthy. Fortunately, through therapy, I learned and accepted that I deserved to have a good time. Outside of Viola getting seasick on the very night of the captain's dinner, everything about our seven day Caribbean cruise was spectacular!

Herman and Viola during the Captains Dinner.

▲ ▲ ▲

One very important component to my continued recovery of PTSD was taking advantage of the VA's vocational rehabilitation program (VHP). This program started where the twelve week psychotherapy program ended. The purpose of the VHP program was to supply a totally disabled veteran with the tools for his hobby to make his life enjoyable. Since high school, I'd had a strong interest in radio and TV repair, and since I had become a totally disabled veteran, on account of my physical wounds and invisible wound, VHP helped fund my equipment. Subsequently, I set up a TV repair workshop in my garage. I figure my TV repair work fits somewhere in between a hobby and a business with no boss to scrutinize my work, and no time clocks to punch. When I can't sleep, I can go out to my workshop even if its 3:00 a.m. It really gives me a sense of accomplishment to take a malfunctioned TV or radio and bring it back to life.

CHAPTER 38

∧ ∧ ∧

OVER THE YEARS, my relationship with my biological mother, Cora Mae, continued to flourish. She still lived in Warren, Ohio, but occasionally made visits at my home in Cleveland, Ohio. Our oldest son, Maurice, had grown up and moved to his own apartment, and after Cora spent a couple weeks at my home, she then went over to Maurice's and stayed with him for a spell.

Like many people who start their small business at home, Maurice began his barber business, cutting hair right in our kitchen. That is, until his mother made him relocate to the basement. As a barber, he was privileged to have several members of the Cleveland Browns football team as his patrons. He introduced Cora Mae and me to players such as Eddie Johnson and Bernie Kosar. I really appreciated the time that they allowed us to hang out with them.

Meeting these players also made it possible to arrange for some of the other players on the team to visit the PTSD patients at the VA during the holidays and sign autographs. During those visits, the patients would straighten up and be on their very best behavior.

After spending a couple of weeks with Maurice, Cora Mae returned to her home in Warren, Ohio. Not long afterwards, I got the call that I needed to come to the hospital right away. I jumped in the car and sped down I-80. Driving at record breaking speed, I arrived within an hour, in time to see my mother wired up to a respirator. She had suffered a stroke. I said what I needed to say to her and shortly thereafter, on February 19, 1994, she took her last breath. Similarly, my mother's husband, Amos, passed away a couple years prior, also due to a stroke.

My father, James Small, passed away on August 1, 1994, the same year as Cora Mae. When I drove to Columbus, Ohio, to visit him at University Hospital, his stomach was still opened up. I'm not sure of the actual cause of his death. Although my father has passed on, I am fortunate that my stepmother Ruby is still in my life.

CHAPTER 39

▲ ▲ ▲

ON ONE OF my visits to George's office, our conversation, as it so often did, transitioned from my current legal snafu to my many experiences at the VA. The subject of "good" customer service was a constant source of contention amongst us veterans. In fact, there was a time when we actually thought the doctors and therapists were afraid of us. Whether it was our paranoia, another common symptom of PTSD, or whether the doctors even realized their lack of a compassionate bedside manner, it was real in the minds of us veterans. As a result of this conversation, George spoke to his wife, Victoria, and encouraged her to extend an invite for me to address the interns at the podiatry college. I don't think Victoria could have predicted how much of a benefit this opportunity would present when she obliged.

Standing before the interns, I spilled my guts. I asked my audience to reflect back to age nineteen and recall what they were doing. I'm sure many were doing the average things that teenagers do such as drinking, experimenting with drugs and sex. I then went on to tell them that the average age of the soldiers in Vietnam was nineteen and what we as soldiers were doing. At that young age, we were being shot at, at every turn, eating C-rations from a can, sleeping on the ground amid high grass, barely tolerating intensive temperatures of over 120 degrees, no running water for bathing, digging holes in the ground as venues for our human waste and seeing our friends killed in action, some actually mutilated. Simply devastating! This is the type of daily life soldiers experienced. Being that we were in the military, whether we enlisted voluntarily, or were conscripted by the draft, once in uniform, most served our country with honor. We would greatly appreciate being treated with dignity and respect when we come to the VA.

I can honestly say that after I spoke to Victoria's interns, customer service improved tremendously for me *and* the other veterans. For weeks after, whenever I walked through Wade Park VA, staff would shake my hand and made positive comments about my speech. Prior to then, the receptionist used to rush me out the door as soon as I made my exit from the doctor's office. You would have thought I had a disease that she didn't want to catch. Now, she takes time to ask how I'm feeling. I felt like a human being, and not someone with a disorder that made the very people in the position to help me, be afraid of me. I will forever thank Victoria for that opportunity to speak to her group of interns.

▲ ▲ ▲

On another visit to George's office, I was reliving my demolition training in Vietnam and the subsequent explosion that I performed. From that day on, George fondly nicknamed me "The Hermanator."

CHAPTER 40

▲ ▲ ▲

IN 2002, TWELVE years after I first entered the PTSD program, I was chosen to attend a Veterans Administration conference in Memphis, Tennessee, for the purpose of developing a peer support program for veterans. It was truly an honor to be in the presence of care givers from all over the country. Also in attendance was a VA attorney from Washington, D.C., and a host of mental health care representatives from all over the United States. Since I was the first veteran from the Cleveland area to participate in the first training of "Understanding Peer Support," I became known as "Peer One."

Following the conference, the therapist who I accompanied, returned to the VA fully charged and excited about implementing the program. We were both excited. Subsequent to the training, Brecksville, near Cleveland, became the first VA facility to create the "Vet to Vet" model of care in Ohio.

As a peer support facilitator and being actively engaged in my own personal recovery, I received training to help others identify and achieve life and recovery goals for themselves. I gained a new level of understanding of what it means to struggle with mental health or substance abuse issues.

Aside from assisting veterans at the VA medical center, my past work experience at the federal building has also yielded some knowledge that allows me to assist veterans in need of various other services offered by the Department of Veterans Affairs.

What is peer support?

Peer support has been used for years to assist people with medical illnesses or addictions. More recently, peer support has been used within mental health services to assist people in their recovery from mental health problems.

The basic idea is that Veterans who have been successful in their recovery from mental health or substance abuse problems have a lot to offer, especially to Veterans who are newer to VA mental health services. In the VA, who would be a better peer than another Veteran?

I am honored to make presentations to new groups of veterans who've been diagnosed with chronic PTSD and are committed to participate in the twelve weeks of psychotherapy and treatment. During orientation, (pictured in the brochure) I emphasize to the veteran, "You were not born with PTSD. This disorder was acquired due to the trauma you faced during your military combat service. Certain triggers will bring it all back, so as long as you're alive, you are subject to the demons of PTSD. However, you can live with it and with specialized treatment, you will learn how to better cope. Once you understand you're not *crazy*, and you have nothing to be ashamed of, you're on the road to recovery."

Each time I speak with new veterans at the CSR, I feel like I'm speaking through the souls of the dead whose names appear on the Vietnam Veterans Memorial Wall in Washington, D. C.

About midway through the twelve week program, I meet with the group once more. This is a critical time during their recovery. In the past, many veterans have dealt with their traumas by drug use, alcohol, isolation and more. Now they are receiving psychotherapy, a new and different way of dealing with their traumas. I let them know that I've been through what they've been through and I'm going through what they're going through. If I can make it, they can too.

▲ ▲ ▲

As I walk through the Wade Park VA center today, many veterans wave with recognition. They know me from the past when they needed encouragement and I was there to give them that extra boost to get through. We veterans realize that the same doctors are not going to be with us forever. We'll be lucky to have the same one for a year, or maybe as long as two years, but, as long as my Creator allows me to, I'll be there. Chances are, my path will cross with another veteran at one time or another down the road at the VA. For them to see a veteran like me who has been involved with my recovery for as long as I have, they know that I'm serious and they can count on me to help in any way I can. My reputation about being serious is for real.

▲ ▲ ▲

Under the new model of the peer support program, I have accompanied some of the new veterans to a mock funeral, another therapeutic experience offered at the Ohio Western Reserve National Cemetery, in Rittman, Ohio. The mock funeral is presented with the 21 gun salute. Every veteran is offered this experience at the tail end of the twelve weeks before graduating from the program. Initially, many veterans had a conflict with this experience, but were given a few weeks to prepare themselves. In the end, it was more than a suggestion that they participate. By the time the mock funerals were incorporated into the program, I had become a peer support facilitator. But, like the other veterans taking part in the ceremony, it helped us all to bring closure to someone we've lost.

CHAPTER 41

——— ▲ ▲ ▲ ———

DURING THE WINTER of 2004, I responded to a request from George to stop by his office. He surprised me with the news that he was planning to retire and move from Cleveland, Ohio, to Seattle, Washington. "What?" I replied, not ready to lose my friend and attorney. "Man, Seattle is quite a long way," I said. "There's even about a three hour difference in the time zone, right?"

"Yes, it's quite a distance," George nodded. "By car, it will take you about thirty-five hours. However, flight time is only about four hours."

I sat across from George's desk as he continued to share his plans to relocate which surprisingly included me. "To start, I'd like you to take the drive with me cross country." I couldn't believe my ears that this man wanted to continue our friendship even across the many miles between Ohio and Washington. He was sincere, indeed.

▲ ▲ ▲

In May, 2005, George and I piled into his Mercedes SUV. When we started out, I simply thought I was helping him drive his vehicle across the country to his new home. Boy, did he have a surprise for me. We drove so many miles each day then stopped to take in a few tourist attractions along the way. In Montana, we stopped at Yellowstone National Park and saw one of the world's most famous geysers. See picture below.

In addition to the volcanic geyser, we came up close and personal with a bison. George tried to bribe me with a measly $50 to climb aboard and straddle one of those four legged beasts that run free in the wilderness of the park.

But, to his ridiculous bribe, I raised the stakes. "Add an extra $50 and I'll kiss it too!"

I'm still in awe today over the fascinating calcite formations, of which I'd never even heard of such prior to George taking me to the Jewel Cave. There's definitely something magical about the way they sparkle. Jewel Cave is the third longest cave in the world and is located in the Black Hills of South Dakota. George and I actually took an elevator down into the cave. I don't remember how many feet we went down into the earth, but it was a *long* way down. My experience was absolutely, awesome!

We also visited Mount Rushmore and saw the face sculptures of U.S. Presidents: George Washington; Thomas Jefferson; Theodore Roosevelt and Abraham Lincoln.

From the balcony of George's lovely new home, we sat and enjoyed our breakfast while admiring the view of Mount Rainier, the highest mountain in the United States.

Mount Rainier is an active stratovolcano, dangerous, but breathtaking. It crossed my mind while sitting on George's balcony that God might be allowing me to see this spectacular sight because he was preparing me for death.

Truly, George renewed my faith in humanity, and of course, my trust in him soared through the roof.

For several years after, I made an annual trip to Seattle to visit with George and his family. Each trip was like a gigantic pool of therapy, filled with a lifetime of extraordinary memories, such as attending my first rotary club meeting, attending my first symphony and more. In between visits, I occasionally pull out the photos of our road trip, just to recharge my spirit.

Even now, with the long distance between us, George and I still maintain a close bond. He's like a brother to me, like Schwarzenegger and DeVito, separated at birth. I am honored to be called, Uncle Herman, by his kids, Gabriella and Wyatt.

Pictured above, Victoria with Wyatt in her arms,
George with Gabriella in his arms and Herman.

CHAPTER 42

▲ ▲ ▲

A BREAKTHROUGH IN a new therapy, "Prolonged Exposure," was introduced about twenty years after I'd gone through the PTSD program four separate times. Anita, my therapist, had just returned from a training class in Atlanta, Georgia. "This is going to be tough," she'd warned. "But, I'm hopeful it may offer a breakthrough for you."

"I'm serious about my recovery and ready to try any and all therapies, as long as we avoid drugs. I'm not doing any more drugs!" Over the years, during my stay at Brecksville, I'd sampled trazodone, nefazodone, amitriptyline and thorazine, all psychotic medications designed to calm me down. None of these proved to be beneficial to my recovery. For me, psychotherapy and group therapy have provided the better results.

"I assure you," Anita replied. "Prolonged exposure is not a drug." She dimmed the lights and started the tape recorder. Like hypnosis, I relived moments in the battlefield with clarity. I even divulged the actual names of my fellow marines, a miraculous feat since I couldn't remember but a few names prior to the prolonged exposure treatment. Amazingly, I could even smell the land (bush) in Vietnam. It was awesome! Anita had been right. It was a breakthrough. As I listened to the tape after the session, I was amazed to hear with my own two ears, myself recalling information I'd long suppressed. A copy of the taped recording was sent to Atlanta for reference to the study.

CHAPTER 43

 ▲▲▲

TODAY, I ATTEND group therapy on the senior level, two to three times a month. A therapist is in attendance during the first twenty minutes, after which the veterans in the group proceed to process ourselves and discuss matters that have occurred since the last visit.

One of the VA doctors once apologized to me. "We, meaning myself and the other psychologists, forget that you are a patient. As a peer facilitator, Herman, you help so many veterans, and in so doing, you help us help veterans, as well."

"Doc, when I help others, it helps me too. Until there is a magic pill that can take PTSD away for good, you can count on me to be here offering any assistance I can to my fellow veterans."

C H A P T E R   4 4

———— ▲ ▲ ▲ ————

DURING THIS BOOK writing project, my book writer requested that I obtain a copy of my VA records to verify information pertinent for my story. Believe me, this was no easy feat to accomplish. First, filling out paperwork with the VA is like that saying, "nothing is as easy as it seems" and it's even twice the work with the VA.

Secondly, I was a little nervous about the information that I'd find in those old records. After all, that was forty-nine years ago. However, realizing the importance of providing accurate information in my autobiography, I complied.

I submitted the first request for my VA records and was told the turnaround time would take up to twelve weeks. Upon the twelfth week, I began checking the mailbox daily. Each time I sorted through the pile of envelopes, there was no denying the anxiety building up inside.

When the fourteenth week passed and still no records had arrived, I made a visit to the regional VA office to find out the status. To my utter disappointment, I was told that my first request was never received and therefore, it would take another twelve weeks. Disappointed? Yes. Surprised?

No. I could back-up this fact about the VA with more stories, but that would take another book.

Again, I began the count down and true to their word, *this time*, the records arrived around the twelfth week. Finally, with the envelope in hand, I was elated, at first. As I started to read through the huge stack of documents, I felt like I was at the VA going through one of the prolonged exposure sessions. My combat history, locations of missions and operations, data regarding my wounds, it all took me back to the killing fields of Vietnam.

Reading further, I noticed the phrase, *readymade family,* which hit me hard. This reference was documented about my living arrangement with Viola prior to our marriage. It also made me recall one of my therapist who once said that *many* soldiers married women with children, creating an already made family. PTSD victims often experience a tremendous amount of guilt on account of the "fog of war." If I listen to anti-war protestors, they'd have me believe I was a murderer who committed atrocities of my own free will. Believe me, in the years prior to treatment, the idea stayed in my psyche far too long. However, thanks to therapy, I can morally defend my actions because I was serving in my role in the United States Marine Corps - simply obeying my orders.

Like many PTSD veterans, trauma often creates physical changes in our brain and our ability to think clearly is hampered. When I met Viola, she was a divorcee with four young children and no permanent father figure in their lives. I believed I had enough love in my heart to take care of them. At the same time, is it possible that helping them has helped me to overcome the pain and guilt I suffered from being called a "baby killer?" In spite of this positive theory, there is a flip side that I cannot deny. My having PTSD has caused my wife and children to suffer. I often struggle with guilt over that. Was I a blessing, or was I a curse to Viola and her children? This question has crossed my mind often.

CHAPTER 45

▲ ▲ ▲

THE VIETNAM WAR lasted twenty years, (1955-1975). The average age of the soldiers who fought in the Vietnam War was nineteen. Approximately 2,700,000 baby boomers participated in the Vietnam War, and more than 50,000 lost their lives. Less than 850,000 are estimated to be alive today. Thanks to my Divine Creator, I am one.

I found it very interesting to learn that the state with the highest death rate was my home state, West Virginia, with 84.1% (national average 58.9% for every 100,000 males in 1970).

Statistics were taken from a variety of sources to include: The VFW Magazine, the Public Information Office, and the HQ CP Forward Observer - 1st Recon April 12, 1997, Sobering Statistics, and History-World.org/vietnam_war_ statistics.htm.

▲ ▲ ▲

Today, as of this writing, there is no known cure for PTSD. We can only hope that a cure is just over the horizon. To contribute in that effort, I am considering donating my brain to a PTSD Brain Bank after my death. The initial phone call has been made and I've ordered brochures for my family to better understand the process.

Since the VA has funded the National Posttraumatic Stress Disorder (PTSD Brain Bank), and as a recipient of many benefits offered by the VA over the years, I feel compelled to give back. Realizing that my body will be cold in the ground before my brain can even be used, I hope it will warm the hearts of my family to know that my donation may help future efforts in the research, treatment and cure of PTSD. That is, if a cure has not been found prior to my death.

In the meantime, I still reside in Cleveland, Ohio, with my wife, Viola, and together we live a full life. I admit, the compulsion to travel is still apparent from time to time, but those urges to pack up and relocate are long gone. I now enjoy vacations with my wife, and we travel making regular visits to see family members and friends.

Viola continues to wait on the sidelines for a breakthrough in medical science to cure PTSD, as well. Then perhaps she can put away the wooden backscratcher that she keeps close at the ready to defend herself from my kicks, which occur during my sporadic nightmares.

▲ ▲ ▲

During my quest to cope and recover from PTSD, I have evolved from in-patient, to out-patient, to peer support facilitator at the Louis Stokes VA Medical Center in Cleveland,

Ohio, where I currently offer my assistance to fellow veterans seeking to cope with PTSD. I thoroughly enjoy my role as peer support facilitator. I consider it a privilege to speak to new groups of veterans who've been diagnosed with chronic PTSD and have made a commitment to attend the twelve week program for psychotherapy and treatment.

As *one of them* who also suffers from PTSD, I am a living testimony to the other veterans that they can make it through the program, just like I did. They can also improve their lives and learn to cope with PTSD, just like I have.

Serving as peer support facilitator is very rewarding for both veteran and me. I can help dispel those doubts that creep into the minds of a veteran which makes it hard to seek help. For many, there is a looming question behind the very idea of speaking with a therapist. "How can you help me, when you haven't been where I've been?" Veterans helping veterans is the key.

As often as I can, I attend events like the following:

- Annual D-Day Conneaut - Conneaut, Ohio
- Amherst American Legion Dinner - Amherst, Ohio
- Military Air Preservation Society (MAPS) Museum - Canton, Ohio, held annually to celebrate and welcome troops
- Traveling Mini Vietnam Wall which allows attendees to walk up and touch
- Tour of Titan Aircraft - Where Dreams Take Flight - Austinburg, Ohio
- Various annual Veterans Day events

On occasion, I also accept invitations to speak at various veterans events. It was during one of those events that I reconnected with Sam Felton, a former veteran who I hadn't seen for twenty years. Sam and I shared a room at the VA in Brecksville, Ohio.

Purple Hearts and PTSD

Vietnam, Iraq Marines come together at American Legion Post 118

By Jason Hawk
jhawk@civitasmedia.com

For someone with such gentle eyes, Herman Williams has stories to chill the soul.

In a quiet voice, he told last Tuesday of his time in Vietnam, of seeing his best friend killed, of having his entire battalion wiped out, of dealing with the demons of his own actions while in uniform, including "an episode" that led to the death of a Vietnamese baby.

There were also the war protests he found on return to the United States.

"It was crazy," he said. "We'd just been through the worst any person could imagine. When my plane came in.

Herman Williams, Sam Felton Jr. and Collin Smith come together at American Legion Post 118 in Amherst. Williams, who served in Vietnam, has three Purple Hearts. Felton, also a Vietnam veteran, has two Purple Hearts and holds the Navy Cross. Smith, an Iraq War veteran, received one Purple Heart. All have wrestled with PTSD.

Above article and photo published in the Amherst News-Times. I am pictured alongside Sam Felton and Collin Smith. Sam received two Purple Hearts for the wounds he sustained during the Vietnam War. Collin, an Iraq War veteran, received one Purple Heart.

I also had the honor of being published in the Wall Street Journal, issue date November 29, 2014. Article is illustrated on back book cover.

During a 2016, Veterans Day Ceremony in Oberlin, Ohio, I was one of several speakers who addressed the audience. Following is a snapshot of my remarks as published in the Oberlin News Tribune captioned: VETERANS DAY

SPEAKERS CALL FOR EMPATHY, UNITY IN DIVIDED NATION:

Herman Williams, a U.S. Marine and Vietnam War veteran, said he was wounded three times and came home with post-traumatic stress disorder. Now a peer support facilitator with the VA in Cleveland, he told the audience he's grateful for the respect shown veterans at the ceremony and would mention it to those he works with who have PTSD.

Williams said after the ceremony that he worries that the VA — criticized by Trump for failing to provide care in a timely fashion — may be privatized. Trump's 10-point campaign plan regarding veterans doesn't call for privatization but would allow veterans to get care at a "private service provider of their choice."

The plan also calls for making it easier to discipline and fire incompetent VA employees. However, Williams said the VA is getting a bum rap.

More than half of the 1.56 million veterans who've returned from the Afghanistan and Iraq wars sought care through the VA, according to a 2013 study by Harvard economist Linda Bilmes, who analyzed Department of Defense statistics. Half of Afghanistan and Iraq vets have applied for permanent disability benefits, according to the study. One-third have mental illness including anxiety, depression and PTSD, and 253,000 have traumatic brain injuries.

"There's some horror stories, but there a lot of good," Williams said of VA care. "The VA is working harder to do better."

▲ ▲ ▲

Finally, thanks to my book writer, Wyvonne Page of Page Turners, LLC, who has offered her service with this endeavor as a "labor of love," in appreciation for my military service in the U.S. Marine Corps. Truly her invaluable service is not only appreciated; I am extremely grateful.

46392886R00129

Made in the USA
Middletown, DE
30 July 2017